The Pri̶

Baron Alfred Tennyson Tennyson

Alpha Editions

This edition published in 2024

ISBN 9789362093097

Design and Setting By

Alpha Editions

www.alphaedis.com

Email - info@alphaedis.com

Contents

PROLOGUE

Sir Walter Vivian all a summer's day
Gave his broad lawns until the set of sun
Up to the people: thither flocked at noon
His tenants, wife and child, and thither half
The neighbouring borough with their Institute
Of which he was the patron. I was there
From college, visiting the son,—the son
A Walter too,—with others of our set,
Five others: we were seven at Vivian-place.

And me that morning Walter showed the house,
Greek, set with busts: from vases in the hall
Flowers of all heavens, and lovelier than their names,
Grew side by side; and on the pavement lay
Carved stones of the Abbey-ruin in the park,
Huge Ammonites, and the first bones of Time;
And on the tables every clime and age
Jumbled together; celts and calumets,
Claymore and snowshoe, toys in lava, fans
Of sandal, amber, ancient rosaries,
Laborious orient ivory sphere in sphere,
The cursed Malayan crease, and battle-clubs
From the isles of palm: and higher on the walls,
Betwixt the monstrous horns of elk and deer,
His own forefathers' arms and armour hung.

And 'this' he said 'was Hugh's at Agincourt;
And that was old Sir Ralph's at Ascalon:
A good knight he! we keep a chronicle
With all about him'—which he brought, and I
Dived in a hoard of tales that dealt with knights,
Half-legend, half-historic, counts and kings
Who laid about them at their wills and died;
And mixt with these, a lady, one that armed
Her own fair head, and sallying through the gate,
Had beat her foes with slaughter from her walls.

'O miracle of women,' said the book,
'O noble heart who, being strait-besieged
By this wild king to force her to his wish,
Nor bent, nor broke, nor shunned a soldier's death,
But now when all was lost or seemed as lost—
Her stature more than mortal in the burst
Of sunrise, her arm lifted, eyes on fire—
Brake with a blast of trumpets from the gate,
And, falling on them like a thunderbolt,
She trampled some beneath her horses' heels,
And some were whelmed with missiles of the wall,
And some were pushed with lances from the rock,
And part were drowned within the whirling brook:
O miracle of noble womanhood!'

So sang the gallant glorious chronicle;
And, I all rapt in this, 'Come out,' he said,
'To the Abbey: there is Aunt Elizabeth

And sister Lilia with the rest.' We went
(I kept the book and had my finger in it)
Down through the park: strange was the sight to me;
For all the sloping pasture murmured, sown
With happy faces and with holiday.
There moved the multitude, a thousand heads:
The patient leaders of their Institute
Taught them with facts. One reared a font of stone
And drew, from butts of water on the slope,
The fountain of the moment, playing, now
A twisted snake, and now a rain of pearls,
Or steep-up spout whereon the gilded ball
Danced like a wisp: and somewhat lower down
A man with knobs and wires and vials fired
A cannon: Echo answered in her sleep
From hollow fields: and here were telescopes
For azure views; and there a group of girls
In circle waited, whom the electric shock
Dislinked with shrieks and laughter: round the lake
A little clock-work steamer paddling plied
And shook the lilies: perched about the knolls
A dozen angry models jetted steam:
A petty railway ran: a fire-balloon
Rose gem-like up before the dusky groves
And dropt a fairy parachute and past:
And there through twenty posts of telegraph
They flashed a saucy message to and fro
Between the mimic stations; so that sport
Went hand in hand with Science; otherwhere

Pure sport; a herd of boys with clamour bowled
And stumped the wicket; babies rolled about
Like tumbled fruit in grass; and men and maids
Arranged a country dance, and flew through light
And shadow, while the twangling violin
Struck up with Soldier-laddie, and overhead
The broad ambrosial aisles of lofty lime
Made noise with bees and breeze from end to end.

Strange was the sight and smacking of the time;
And long we gazed, but satiated at length
Came to the ruins. High-arched and ivy-claspt,
Of finest Gothic lighter than a fire,
Through one wide chasm of time and frost they gave
The park, the crowd, the house; but all within
The sward was trim as any garden lawn:
And here we lit on Aunt Elizabeth,
And Lilia with the rest, and lady friends
From neighbour seats: and there was Ralph himself,
A broken statue propt against the wall,
As gay as any. Lilia, wild with sport,
Half child half woman as she was, had wound
A scarf of orange round the stony helm,
And robed the shoulders in a rosy silk,
That made the old warrior from his ivied nook
Glow like a sunbeam: near his tomb a feast
Shone, silver-set; about it lay the guests,
And there we joined them: then the maiden Aunt
Took this fair day for text, and from it preached

An universal culture for the crowd,
And all things great; but we, unworthier, told
Of college: he had climbed across the spikes,
And he had squeezed himself betwixt the bars,
And he had breathed the Proctor's dogs; and one
Discussed his tutor, rough to common men,
But honeying at the whisper of a lord;
And one the Master, as a rogue in grain
Veneered with sanctimonious theory.
But while they talked, above their heads I saw
The feudal warrior lady-clad; which brought
My book to mind: and opening this I read
Of old Sir Ralph a page or two that rang
With tilt and tourney; then the tale of her
That drove her foes with slaughter from her walls,
And much I praised her nobleness, and 'Where,'
Asked Walter, patting Lilia's head (she lay
Beside him) 'lives there such a woman now?'

Quick answered Lilia 'There are thousands now
Such women, but convention beats them down:
It is but bringing up; no more than that:
You men have done it: how I hate you all!
Ah, were I something great! I wish I were
Some might poetess, I would shame you then,
That love to keep us children! O I wish
That I were some great princess, I would build
Far off from men a college like a man's,
And I would teach them all that men are taught;

- 5 -

We are twice as quick!' And here she shook aside
The hand that played the patron with her curls.

And one said smiling 'Pretty were the sight
If our old halls could change their sex, and flaunt
With prudes for proctors, dowagers for deans,
And sweet girl-graduates in their golden hair.
I think they should not wear our rusty gowns,
But move as rich as Emperor-moths, or Ralph
Who shines so in the corner; yet I fear,
If there were many Lilias in the brood,
However deep you might embower the nest,
Some boy would spy it.'
At this upon the sward
She tapt her tiny silken-sandaled foot:
'That's your light way; but I would make it death
For any male thing but to peep at us.'

Petulant she spoke, and at herself she laughed;
A rosebud set with little wilful thorns,
And sweet as English air could make her, she:
But Walter hailed a score of names upon her,
And 'petty Ogress', and 'ungrateful Puss',
And swore he longed at college, only longed,
All else was well, for she-society.
They boated and they cricketed; they talked
At wine, in clubs, of art, of politics;
They lost their weeks; they vext the souls of deans;
They rode; they betted; made a hundred friends,

And caught the blossom of the flying terms,
But missed the mignonette of Vivian-place,
The little hearth-flower Lilia. Thus he spoke,
Part banter, part affection.
'True,' she said,
'We doubt not that. O yes, you missed us much.
I'll stake my ruby ring upon it you did.'

She held it out; and as a parrot turns
Up through gilt wires a crafty loving eye,
And takes a lady's finger with all care,
And bites it for true heart and not for harm,
So he with Lilia's. Daintily she shrieked
And wrung it. 'Doubt my word again!' he said.
'Come, listen! here is proof that you were missed:
We seven stayed at Christmas up to read;
And there we took one tutor as to read:
The hard-grained Muses of the cube and square
Were out of season: never man, I think,
So mouldered in a sinecure as he:
For while our cloisters echoed frosty feet,
And our long walks were stript as bare as brooms,
We did but talk you over, pledge you all
In wassail; often, like as many girls—
Sick for the hollies and the yews of home—
As many little trifling Lilias—played
Charades and riddles as at Christmas here,
And what's my thought and when and where and how,
As here at Christmas.'

She remembered that:

A pleasant game, she thought: she liked it more

Than magic music, forfeits, all the rest.

But these—what kind of tales did men tell men,

She wondered, by themselves?

A half-disdain

Perched on the pouted blossom of her lips:

And Walter nodded at me; 'He began,

The rest would follow, each in turn; and so

We forged a sevenfold story. Kind? what kind?

Chimeras, crotchets, Christmas solecisms,

Seven-headed monsters only made to kill

Time by the fire in winter.'

'Kill him now,

The tyrant! kill him in the summer too,'

Said Lilia; 'Why not now?' the maiden Aunt.

'Why not a summer's as a winter's tale?

A tale for summer as befits the time,

And something it should be to suit the place,

Heroic, for a hero lies beneath,

Grave, solemn!'

Walter warped his mouth at this

To something so mock-solemn, that I laughed

And Lilia woke with sudden-thrilling mirth

An echo like a ghostly woodpecker,

Hid in the ruins; till the maiden Aunt

(A little sense of wrong had touched her face

With colour) turned to me with 'As you will;

Heroic if you will, or what you will,

Or be yourself you hero if you will.'

'Take Lilia, then, for heroine' clamoured he,
'And make her some great Princess, six feet high,
Grand, epic, homicidal; and be you
The Prince to win her!'
'Then follow me, the Prince,'
I answered, 'each be hero in his turn!
Seven and yet one, like shadows in a dream.—
Heroic seems our Princess as required—
But something made to suit with Time and place,
A Gothic ruin and a Grecian house,
A talk of college and of ladies' rights,
A feudal knight in silken masquerade,
And, yonder, shrieks and strange experiments
For which the good Sir Ralph had burnt them all—
This were a medley! we should have him back
Who told the "Winter's tale" to do it for us.
No matter: we will say whatever comes.
And let the ladies sing us, if they will,
From time to time, some ballad or a song
To give us breathing-space.'
So I began,
And the rest followed: and the women sang
Between the rougher voices of the men,
Like linnets in the pauses of the wind:
And here I give the story and the songs.

I

A prince I was, blue-eyed, and fair in face,
Of temper amorous, as the first of May,
With lengths of yellow ringlet, like a girl,
For on my cradle shone the Northern star.

There lived an ancient legend in our house.
Some sorcerer, whom a far-off grandsire burnt
Because he cast no shadow, had foretold,
Dying, that none of all our blood should know
The shadow from the substance, and that one
Should come to fight with shadows and to fall.
For so, my mother said, the story ran.
And, truly, waking dreams were, more or less,
An old and strange affection of the house.
Myself too had weird seizures, Heaven knows what:
On a sudden in the midst of men and day,
And while I walked and talked as heretofore,
I seemed to move among a world of ghosts,
And feel myself the shadow of a dream.
Our great court-Galen poised his gilt-head cane,
And pawed his beard, and muttered 'catalepsy'.
My mother pitying made a thousand prayers;
My mother was as mild as any saint,
Half-canonized by all that looked on her,
So gracious was her tact and tenderness:
But my good father thought a king a king;

He cared not for the affection of the house;
He held his sceptre like a pedant's wand
To lash offence, and with long arms and hands
Reached out, and picked offenders from the mass
For judgment.
Now it chanced that I had been,
While life was yet in bud and blade, bethrothed
To one, a neighbouring Princess: she to me
Was proxy-wedded with a bootless calf
At eight years old; and still from time to time
Came murmurs of her beauty from the South,
And of her brethren, youths of puissance;
And still I wore her picture by my heart,
And one dark tress; and all around them both
Sweet thoughts would swarm as bees about their queen.

But when the days drew nigh that I should wed,
My father sent ambassadors with furs
And jewels, gifts, to fetch her: these brought back
A present, a great labour of the loom;
And therewithal an answer vague as wind:
Besides, they saw the king; he took the gifts;
He said there was a compact; that was true:
But then she had a will; was he to blame?
And maiden fancies; loved to live alone
Among her women; certain, would not wed.

That morning in the presence room I stood
With Cyril and with Florian, my two friends:

The first, a gentleman of broken means
(His father's fault) but given to starts and bursts
Of revel; and the last, my other heart,
And almost my half-self, for still we moved
Together, twinned as horse's ear and eye.

Now, while they spake, I saw my father's face
Grow long and troubled like a rising moon,
Inflamed with wrath: he started on his feet,
Tore the king's letter, snowed it down, and rent
The wonder of the loom through warp and woof
From skirt to skirt; and at the last he sware
That he would send a hundred thousand men,
And bring her in a whirlwind: then he chewed
The thrice-turned cud of wrath, and cooked his spleen,
Communing with his captains of the war.

At last I spoke. 'My father, let me go.
It cannot be but some gross error lies
In this report, this answer of a king,
Whom all men rate as kind and hospitable:
Or, maybe, I myself, my bride once seen,
Whate'er my grief to find her less than fame,
May rue the bargain made.' And Florian said:
'I have a sister at the foreign court,
Who moves about the Princess; she, you know,
Who wedded with a nobleman from thence:
He, dying lately, left her, as I hear,
The lady of three castles in that land:

Through her this matter might be sifted clean.'
And Cyril whispered: 'Take me with you too.'
Then laughing 'what, if these weird seizures come
Upon you in those lands, and no one near
To point you out the shadow from the truth!
Take me: I'll serve you better in a strait;
I grate on rusty hinges here:' but 'No!'
Roared the rough king, 'you shall not; we ourself
Will crush her pretty maiden fancies dead
In iron gauntlets: break the council up.'

But when the council broke, I rose and past
Through the wild woods that hung about the town;
Found a still place, and plucked her likeness out;
Laid it on flowers, and watched it lying bathed
In the green gleam of dewy-tasselled trees:
What were those fancies? wherefore break her troth?
Proud looked the lips: but while I meditated
A wind arose and rushed upon the South,
And shook the songs, the whispers, and the shrieks
Of the wild woods together; and a Voice
Went with it, 'Follow, follow, thou shalt win.'

Then, ere the silver sickle of that month
Became her golden shield, I stole from court
With Cyril and with Florian, unperceived,
Cat-footed through the town and half in dread
To hear my father's clamour at our backs
With Ho! from some bay-window shake the night;

But all was quiet: from the bastioned walls
Like threaded spiders, one by one, we dropt,
And flying reached the frontier: then we crost
To a livelier land; and so by tilth and grange,
And vines, and blowing bosks of wilderness,
We gained the mother city thick with towers,
And in the imperial palace found the king.

His name was Gama; cracked and small his voice,
But bland the smile that like a wrinkling wind
On glassy water drove his cheek in lines;
A little dry old man, without a star,
Not like a king: three days he feasted us,
And on the fourth I spake of why we came,
And my bethrothed. 'You do us, Prince,' he said,
Airing a snowy hand and signet gem,
'All honour. We remember love ourselves
In our sweet youth: there did a compact pass
Long summers back, a kind of ceremony—
I think the year in which our olives failed.
I would you had her, Prince, with all my heart,
With my full heart: but there were widows here,
Two widows, Lady Psyche, Lady Blanche;
They fed her theories, in and out of place
Maintaining that with equal husbandry
The woman were an equal to the man.
They harped on this; with this our banquets rang;
Our dances broke and buzzed in knots of talk;
Nothing but this; my very ears were hot

To hear them: knowledge, so my daughter held,
Was all in all: they had but been, she thought,
As children; they must lose the child, assume
The woman: then, Sir, awful odes she wrote,
Too awful, sure, for what they treated of,
But all she is and does is awful; odes
About this losing of the child; and rhymes
And dismal lyrics, prophesying change
Beyond all reason: these the women sang;
And they that know such things—I sought but peace;
No critic I—would call them masterpieces:
They mastered me. At last she begged a boon,
A certain summer-palace which I have
Hard by your father's frontier: I said no,
Yet being an easy man, gave it: and there,
All wild to found an University
For maidens, on the spur she fled; and more
We know not,—only this: they see no men,
Not even her brother Arac, nor the twins
Her brethren, though they love her, look upon her
As on a kind of paragon; and I
(Pardon me saying it) were much loth to breed
Dispute betwixt myself and mine: but since
(And I confess with right) you think me bound
In some sort, I can give you letters to her;
And yet, to speak the truth, I rate your chance
Almost at naked nothing.'
Thus the king;
And I, though nettled that he seemed to slur

With garrulous ease and oily courtesies
Our formal compact, yet, not less (all frets
But chafing me on fire to find my bride)
Went forth again with both my friends. We rode
Many a long league back to the North. At last
From hills, that looked across a land of hope,
We dropt with evening on a rustic town
Set in a gleaming river's crescent-curve,
Close at the boundary of the liberties;
There, entered an old hostel, called mine host
To council, plied him with his richest wines,
And showed the late-writ letters of the king.

He with a long low sibilation, stared
As blank as death in marble; then exclaimed
Averring it was clear against all rules
For any man to go: but as his brain
Began to mellow, 'If the king,' he said,
'Had given us letters, was he bound to speak?
The king would bear him out;' and at the last—
The summer of the vine in all his veins—
'No doubt that we might make it worth his while.
She once had past that way; he heard her speak;
She scared him; life! he never saw the like;
She looked as grand as doomsday and as grave:
And he, he reverenced his liege-lady there;
He always made a point to post with mares;
His daughter and his housemaid were the boys:
The land, he understood, for miles about

Was tilled by women; all the swine were sows,
And all the dogs'—
But while he jested thus,
A thought flashed through me which I clothed in act,
Remembering how we three presented Maid
Or Nymph, or Goddess, at high tide of feast,
In masque or pageant at my father's court.
We sent mine host to purchase female gear;
He brought it, and himself, a sight to shake
The midriff of despair with laughter, holp
To lace us up, till, each, in maiden plumes
We rustled: him we gave a costly bribe
To guerdon silence, mounted our good steeds,
And boldly ventured on the liberties.

We followed up the river as we rode,
And rode till midnight when the college lights
Began to glitter firefly-like in copse
And linden alley: then we past an arch,
Whereon a woman-statue rose with wings
From four winged horses dark against the stars;
And some inscription ran along the front,
But deep in shadow: further on we gained
A little street half garden and half house;
But scarce could hear each other speak for noise
Of clocks and chimes, like silver hammers falling
On silver anvils, and the splash and stir
Of fountains spouted up and showering down
In meshes of the jasmine and the rose:

And all about us pealed the nightingale,
Rapt in her song, and careless of the snare.

There stood a bust of Pallas for a sign,
By two sphere lamps blazoned like Heaven and Earth
With constellation and with continent,
Above an entry: riding in, we called;
A plump-armed Ostleress and a stable wench
Came running at the call, and helped us down.
Then stept a buxom hostess forth, and sailed,
Full-blown, before us into rooms which gave
Upon a pillared porch, the bases lost
In laurel: her we asked of that and this,
And who were tutors. 'Lady Blanche' she said,
'And Lady Psyche.' 'Which was prettiest,
Best-natured?' 'Lady Psyche.' 'Hers are we,'
One voice, we cried; and I sat down and wrote,
In such a hand as when a field of corn
Bows all its ears before the roaring East;

'Three ladies of the Northern empire pray
Your Highness would enroll them with your own,
As Lady Psyche's pupils.'
This I sealed:
The seal was Cupid bent above a scroll,
And o'er his head Uranian Venus hung,
And raised the blinding bandage from his eyes:
I gave the letter to be sent with dawn;
And then to bed, where half in doze I seemed

To float about a glimmering night, and watch
A full sea glazed with muffled moonlight, swell
On some dark shore just seen that it was rich.

As through the land at eve we went,
And plucked the ripened ears,
We fell out, my wife and I,
O we fell out I know not why,
And kissed again with tears.
And blessings on the falling out
That all the more endears,
When we fall out with those we love
And kiss again with tears!
For when we came where lies the child
We lost in other years,
There above the little grave,
O there above the little grave,
We kissed again with tears.

II

At break of day the College Portress came:
She brought us Academic silks, in hue
The lilac, with a silken hood to each,
And zoned with gold; and now when these were on,
And we as rich as moths from dusk cocoons,
She, curtseying her obeisance, let us know
The Princess Ida waited: out we paced,
I first, and following through the porch that sang
All round with laurel, issued in a court
Compact of lucid marbles, bossed with lengths
Of classic frieze, with ample awnings gay
Betwixt the pillars, and with great urns of flowers.
The Muses and the Graces, grouped in threes,
Enringed a billowing fountain in the midst;
And here and there on lattice edges lay
Or book or lute; but hastily we past,
And up a flight of stairs into the hall.

There at a board by tome and paper sat,
With two tame leopards couched beside her throne,
All beauty compassed in a female form,
The Princess; liker to the inhabitant
Of some clear planet close upon the Sun,
Than our man's earth; such eyes were in her head,
And so much grace and power, breathing down
From over her arched brows, with every turn

Lived through her to the tips of her long hands,
And to her feet. She rose her height, and said:

'We give you welcome: not without redound
Of use and glory to yourselves ye come,
The first-fruits of the stranger: aftertime,
And that full voice which circles round the grave,
Will rank you nobly, mingled up with me.
What! are the ladies of your land so tall?'
'We of the court' said Cyril. 'From the court'
She answered, 'then ye know the Prince?' and he:
'The climax of his age! as though there were
One rose in all the world, your Highness that,
He worships your ideal:' she replied:
'We scarcely thought in our own hall to hear
This barren verbiage, current among men,
Light coin, the tinsel clink of compliment.
Your flight from out your bookless wilds would seem
As arguing love of knowledge and of power;
Your language proves you still the child. Indeed,
We dream not of him: when we set our hand
To this great work, we purposed with ourself
Never to wed. You likewise will do well,
Ladies, in entering here, to cast and fling
The tricks, which make us toys of men, that so,
Some future time, if so indeed you will,
You may with those self-styled our lords ally
Your fortunes, justlier balanced, scale with scale.'

At those high words, we conscious of ourselves,
Perused the matting: then an officer
Rose up, and read the statutes, such as these:
Not for three years to correspond with home;
Not for three years to cross the liberties;
Not for three years to speak with any men;
And many more, which hastily subscribed,
We entered on the boards: and 'Now,' she cried,
'Ye are green wood, see ye warp not. Look, our hall!
Our statues!—not of those that men desire,
Sleek Odalisques, or oracles of mode,
Nor stunted squaws of West or East; but she
That taught the Sabine how to rule, and she
The foundress of the Babylonian wall,
The Carian Artemisia strong in war,
The Rhodope, that built the pyramid,
Clelia, Cornelia, with the Palmyrene
That fought Aurelian, and the Roman brows
Of Agrippina. Dwell with these, and lose
Convention, since to look on noble forms
Makes noble through the sensuous organism
That which is higher. O lift your natures up:
Embrace our aims: work out your freedom. Girls,
Knowledge is now no more a fountain sealed:
Drink deep, until the habits of the slave,
The sins of emptiness, gossip and spite
And slander, die. Better not be at all
Than not be noble. Leave us: you may go:
Today the Lady Psyche will harangue

The fresh arrivals of the week before;
For they press in from all the provinces,
And fill the hive.'
She spoke, and bowing waved
Dismissal: back again we crost the court
To Lady Psyche's: as we entered in,
There sat along the forms, like morning doves
That sun their milky bosoms on the thatch,
A patient range of pupils; she herself
Erect behind a desk of satin-wood,
A quick brunette, well-moulded, falcon-eyed,
And on the hither side, or so she looked,
Of twenty summers. At her left, a child,
In shining draperies, headed like a star,
Her maiden babe, a double April old,
Aglaïa slept. We sat: the Lady glanced:
Then Florian, but not livelier than the dame
That whispered 'Asses' ears', among the sedge,
'My sister.' 'Comely, too, by all that's fair,'
Said Cyril. 'Oh hush, hush!' and she began.

'This world was once a fluid haze of light,
Till toward the centre set the starry tides,
And eddied into suns, that wheeling cast
The planets: then the monster, then the man;
Tattooed or woaded, winter-clad in skins,
Raw from the prime, and crushing down his mate;
As yet we find in barbarous isles, and here
Among the lowest.'

Thereupon she took
A bird's-eye-view of all the ungracious past;
Glanced at the legendary Amazon
As emblematic of a nobler age;
Appraised the Lycian custom, spoke of those
That lay at wine with Lar and Lucumo;
Ran down the Persian, Grecian, Roman lines
Of empire, and the woman's state in each,
How far from just; till warming with her theme
She fulmined out her scorn of laws Salique
And little-footed China, touched on Mahomet
With much contempt, and came to chivalry:
When some respect, however slight, was paid
To woman, superstition all awry:
However then commenced the dawn: a beam
Had slanted forward, falling in a land
Of promise; fruit would follow. Deep, indeed,
Their debt of thanks to her who first had dared
To leap the rotten pales of prejudice,
Disyoke their necks from custom, and assert
None lordlier than themselves but that which made
Woman and man. She had founded; they must build.
Here might they learn whatever men were taught:
Let them not fear: some said their heads were less:
Some men's were small; not they the least of men;
For often fineness compensated size:
Besides the brain was like the hand, and grew
With using; thence the man's, if more was more;
He took advantage of his strength to be

First in the field: some ages had been lost;
But woman ripened earlier, and her life
Was longer; and albeit their glorious names
Were fewer, scattered stars, yet since in truth
The highest is the measure of the man,
And not the Kaffir, Hottentot, Malay,
Nor those horn-handed breakers of the glebe,
But Homer, Plato, Verulam; even so
With woman: and in arts of government
Elizabeth and others; arts of war
The peasant Joan and others; arts of grace
Sappho and others vied with any man:
And, last not least, she who had left her place,
And bowed her state to them, that they might grow
To use and power on this Oasis, lapt
In the arms of leisure, sacred from the blight
Of ancient influence and scorn.
                    At last
She rose upon a wind of prophecy
Dilating on the future; 'everywhere
Who heads in council, two beside the hearth,
Two in the tangled business of the world,
Two in the liberal offices of life,
Two plummets dropt for one to sound the abyss
Of science, and the secrets of the mind:
Musician, painter, sculptor, critic, more:
And everywhere the broad and bounteous Earth
Should bear a double growth of those rare souls,
Poets, whose thoughts enrich the blood of the world.'

She ended here, and beckoned us: the rest
Parted; and, glowing full-faced welcome, she
Began to address us, and was moving on
In gratulation, till as when a boat
Tacks, and the slackened sail flaps, all her voice
Faltering and fluttering in her throat, she cried
'My brother!' 'Well, my sister.' 'O,' she said,
'What do you here? and in this dress? and these?
Why who are these? a wolf within the fold!
A pack of wolves! the Lord be gracious to me!
A plot, a plot, a plot to ruin all!'
'No plot, no plot,' he answered. 'Wretched boy,
How saw you not the inscription on the gate,
LET NO MAN ENTER IN ON PAIN OF DEATH?'
'And if I had,' he answered, 'who could think
The softer Adams of your Academe,
O sister, Sirens though they be, were such
As chanted on the blanching bones of men?'
'But you will find it otherwise' she said.
'You jest: ill jesting with edge-tools! my vow
Binds me to speak, and O that iron will,
That axelike edge unturnable, our Head,
The Princess.' 'Well then, Psyche, take my life,
And nail me like a weasel on a grange
For warning: bury me beside the gate,
And cut this epitaph above my bones;
Here lies a brother by a sister slain,
All for the common good of womankind.'

'Let me die too,' said Cyril, 'having seen
And heard the Lady Psyche.'
I struck in:
'Albeit so masked, Madam, I love the truth;
Receive it; and in me behold the Prince
Your countryman, affianced years ago
To the Lady Ida: here, for here she was,
And thus (what other way was left) I came.'
'O Sir, O Prince, I have no country; none;
If any, this; but none. Whate'er I was
Disrooted, what I am is grafted here.
Affianced, Sir? love-whispers may not breathe
Within this vestal limit, and how should I,
Who am not mine, say, live: the thunderbolt
Hangs silent; but prepare: I speak; it falls.'
'Yet pause,' I said: 'for that inscription there,
I think no more of deadly lurks therein,
Than in a clapper clapping in a garth,
To scare the fowl from fruit: if more there be,
If more and acted on, what follows? war;
Your own work marred: for this your Academe,
Whichever side be Victor, in the halloo
Will topple to the trumpet down, and pass
With all fair theories only made to gild
A stormless summer.' 'Let the Princess judge
Of that' she said: 'farewell, Sir—and to you.
I shudder at the sequel, but I go.'

'Are you that Lady Psyche,' I rejoined,

'The fifth in line from that old Florian,
Yet hangs his portrait in my father's hall
(The gaunt old Baron with his beetle brow
Sun-shaded in the heat of dusty fights)
As he bestrode my Grandsire, when he fell,
And all else fled? we point to it, and we say,
The loyal warmth of Florian is not cold,
But branches current yet in kindred veins.'
'Are you that Psyche,' Florian added; 'she
With whom I sang about the morning hills,
Flung ball, flew kite, and raced the purple fly,
And snared the squirrel of the glen? are you
That Psyche, wont to bind my throbbing brow,
To smoothe my pillow, mix the foaming draught
Of fever, tell me pleasant tales, and read
My sickness down to happy dreams? are you
That brother-sister Psyche, both in one?
You were that Psyche, but what are you now?'
'You are that Psyche,' said Cyril, 'for whom
I would be that for ever which I seem,
Woman, if I might sit beside your feet,
And glean your scattered sapience.'
Then once more,
'Are you that Lady Psyche,' I began,
'That on her bridal morn before she past
From all her old companions, when the kind
Kissed her pale cheek, declared that ancient ties
Would still be dear beyond the southern hills;
That were there any of our people there

In want or peril, there was one to hear
And help them? look! for such are these and I.'
'Are you that Psyche,' Florian asked, 'to whom,
In gentler days, your arrow-wounded fawn
Came flying while you sat beside the well?
The creature laid his muzzle on your lap,
And sobbed, and you sobbed with it, and the blood
Was sprinkled on your kirtle, and you wept.
That was fawn's blood, not brother's, yet you wept.
O by the bright head of my little niece,
You were that Psyche, and what are you now?'
'You are that Psyche,' Cyril said again,
'The mother of the sweetest little maid,
That ever crowed for kisses.'
'Out upon it!'
She answered, 'peace! and why should I not play
The Spartan Mother with emotion, be
The Lucius Junius Brutus of my kind?
Him you call great: he for the common weal,
The fading politics of mortal Rome,
As I might slay this child, if good need were,
Slew both his sons: and I, shall I, on whom
The secular emancipation turns
Of half this world, be swerved from right to save
A prince, a brother? a little will I yield.
Best so, perchance, for us, and well for you.
O hard, when love and duty clash! I fear
My conscience will not count me fleckless; yet—
Hear my conditions: promise (otherwise

- 29 -

You perish) as you came, to slip away

Today, tomorrow, soon: it shall be said,

These women were too barbarous, would not learn;

They fled, who might have shamed us: promise, all.'

What could we else, we promised each; and she,

Like some wild creature newly-caged, commenced

A to-and-fro, so pacing till she paused

By Florian; holding out her lily arms

Took both his hands, and smiling faintly said:

'I knew you at the first: though you have grown

You scarce have altered: I am sad and glad

To see you, Florian. I give thee to death

My brother! it was duty spoke, not I.

My needful seeming harshness, pardon it.

Our mother, is she well?'

With that she kissed

His forehead, then, a moment after, clung

About him, and betwixt them blossomed up

From out a common vein of memory

Sweet household talk, and phrases of the hearth,

And far allusion, till the gracious dews

Began to glisten and to fall: and while

They stood, so rapt, we gazing, came a voice,

'I brought a message here from Lady Blanche.'

Back started she, and turning round we saw

The Lady Blanche's daughter where she stood,

Melissa, with her hand upon the lock,

A rosy blonde, and in a college gown,

That clad her like an April daffodilly
(Her mother's colour) with her lips apart,
And all her thoughts as fair within her eyes,
As bottom agates seen to wave and float
In crystal currents of clear morning seas.

So stood that same fair creature at the door.
Then Lady Psyche, 'Ah—Melissa—you!
You heard us?' and Melissa, 'O pardon me
I heard, I could not help it, did not wish:
But, dearest Lady, pray you fear me not,
Nor think I bear that heart within my breast,
To give three gallant gentlemen to death.'
'I trust you,' said the other, 'for we two
Were always friends, none closer, elm and vine:
But yet your mother's jealous temperament—
Let not your prudence, dearest, drowse, or prove
The Danaïd of a leaky vase, for fear
This whole foundation ruin, and I lose
My honour, these their lives.' 'Ah, fear me not'
Replied Melissa; 'no—I would not tell,
No, not for all Aspasia's cleverness,
No, not to answer, Madam, all those hard things
That Sheba came to ask of Solomon.'
'Be it so' the other, 'that we still may lead
The new light up, and culminate in peace,
For Solomon may come to Sheba yet.'
Said Cyril, 'Madam, he the wisest man
Feasted the woman wisest then, in halls

- 31 -

Of Lebanonian cedar: nor should you
(Though, Madam, you should answer, we would ask)
Less welcome find among us, if you came
Among us, debtors for our lives to you,
Myself for something more.' He said not what,
But 'Thanks,' she answered 'Go: we have been too long
Together: keep your hoods about the face;
They do so that affect abstraction here.
Speak little; mix not with the rest; and hold
Your promise: all, I trust, may yet be well.'

We turned to go, but Cyril took the child,
And held her round the knees against his waist,
And blew the swollen cheek of a trumpeter,
While Psyche watched them, smiling, and the child
Pushed her flat hand against his face and laughed;
And thus our conference closed.
And then we strolled
For half the day through stately theatres
Benched crescent-wise. In each we sat, we heard
The grave Professor. On the lecture slate
The circle rounded under female hands
With flawless demonstration: followed then
A classic lecture, rich in sentiment,
With scraps of thunderous Epic lilted out
By violet-hooded Doctors, elegies
And quoted odes, and jewels five-words-long
That on the stretched forefinger of all Time
Sparkle for ever: then we dipt in all

That treats of whatsoever is, the state,
The total chronicles of man, the mind,
The morals, something of the frame, the rock,
The star, the bird, the fish, the shell, the flower,
Electric, chemic laws, and all the rest,
And whatsoever can be taught and known;
Till like three horses that have broken fence,
And glutted all night long breast-deep in corn,
We issued gorged with knowledge, and I spoke:
'Why, Sirs, they do all this as well as we.'
'They hunt old trails' said Cyril 'very well;
But when did woman ever yet invent?'
'Ungracious!' answered Florian; 'have you learnt
No more from Psyche's lecture, you that talked
The trash that made me sick, and almost sad?'
'O trash' he said, 'but with a kernel in it.
Should I not call her wise, who made me wise?
And learnt? I learnt more from her in a flash,
Than in my brainpan were an empty hull,
And every Muse tumbled a science in.
A thousand hearts lie fallow in these halls,
And round these halls a thousand baby loves
Fly twanging headless arrows at the hearts,
Whence follows many a vacant pang; but O
With me, Sir, entered in the bigger boy,
The Head of all the golden-shafted firm,
The long-limbed lad that had a Psyche too;
He cleft me through the stomacher; and now
What think you of it, Florian? do I chase

The substance or the shadow? will it hold?
I have no sorcerer's malison on me,
No ghostly hauntings like his Highness. I
Flatter myself that always everywhere
I know the substance when I see it. Well,
Are castles shadows? Three of them? Is she
The sweet proprietress a shadow? If not,
Shall those three castles patch my tattered coat?
For dear are those three castles to my wants,
And dear is sister Psyche to my heart,
And two dear things are one of double worth,
And much I might have said, but that my zone
Unmanned me: then the Doctors! O to hear
The Doctors! O to watch the thirsty plants
Imbibing! once or twice I thought to roar,
To break my chain, to shake my mane: but thou,
Modulate me, Soul of mincing mimicry!
Make liquid treble of that bassoon, my throat;
Abase those eyes that ever loved to meet
Star-sisters answering under crescent brows;
Abate the stride, which speaks of man, and loose
A flying charm of blushes o'er this cheek,
Where they like swallows coming out of time
Will wonder why they came: but hark the bell
For dinner, let us go!'
And in we streamed
Among the columns, pacing staid and still
By twos and threes, till all from end to end
With beauties every shade of brown and fair

In colours gayer than the morning mist,

The long hall glittered like a bed of flowers.

How might a man not wander from his wits

Pierced through with eyes, but that I kept mine own

Intent on her, who rapt in glorious dreams,

The second-sight of some Astræan age,

Sat compassed with professors: they, the while,

Discussed a doubt and tost it to and fro:

A clamour thickened, mixt with inmost terms

Of art and science: Lady Blanche alone

Of faded form and haughtiest lineaments,

With all her autumn tresses falsely brown,

Shot sidelong daggers at us, a tiger-cat

In act to spring.

At last a solemn grace

Concluded, and we sought the gardens: there

One walked reciting by herself, and one

In this hand held a volume as to read,

And smoothed a petted peacock down with that:

Some to a low song oared a shallop by,

Or under arches of the marble bridge

Hung, shadowed from the heat: some hid and sought

In the orange thickets: others tost a ball

Above the fountain-jets, and back again

With laughter: others lay about the lawns,

Of the older sort, and murmured that their May

Was passing: what was learning unto them?

They wished to marry; they could rule a house;

Men hated learned women: but we three

Sat muffled like the Fates; and often came
Melissa hitting all we saw with shafts
Of gentle satire, kin to charity,
That harmed not: then day droopt; the chapel bells
Called us: we left the walks; we mixt with those
Six hundred maidens clad in purest white,
Before two streams of light from wall to wall,
While the great organ almost burst his pipes,
Groaning for power, and rolling through the court
A long melodious thunder to the sound
Of solemn psalms, and silver litanies,
The work of Ida, to call down from Heaven
A blessing on her labours for the world.
Sweet and low, sweet and low,
Wind of the western sea,
Low, low, breathe and blow,
Wind of the western sea!
Over the rolling waters go,
Come from the dying moon, and blow,
Blow him again to me;
While my little one, while my pretty one, sleeps.

Sleep and rest, sleep and rest,
Father will come to thee soon;
Rest, rest, on mother's breast,
Father will come to thee soon;
Father will come to his babe in the nest,
Silver sails all out of the west
Under the silver moon:

Sleep, my little one, sleep, my pretty one, sleep.

III

Morn in the wake of the morning star
Came furrowing all the orient into gold.
We rose, and each by other drest with care
Descended to the court that lay three parts
In shadow, but the Muses' heads were touched
Above the darkness from their native East.

There while we stood beside the fount, and watched
Or seemed to watch the dancing bubble, approached
Melissa, tinged with wan from lack of sleep,
Or grief, and glowing round her dewy eyes
The circled Iris of a night of tears;
'And fly,' she cried, 'O fly, while yet you may!
My mother knows:' and when I asked her 'how,'
'My fault' she wept 'my fault! and yet not mine;
Yet mine in part. O hear me, pardon me.
My mother, 'tis her wont from night to night
To rail at Lady Psyche and her side.
She says the Princess should have been the Head,
Herself and Lady Psyche the two arms;
And so it was agreed when first they came;
But Lady Psyche was the right hand now,
And the left, or not, or seldom used;
Hers more than half the students, all the love.
And so last night she fell to canvass you:
Her countrywomen! she did not envy her.

"Who ever saw such wild barbarians?
Girls?—more like men!" and at these words the snake,
My secret, seemed to stir within my breast;
And oh, Sirs, could I help it, but my cheek
Began to burn and burn, and her lynx eye
To fix and make me hotter, till she laughed:
"O marvellously modest maiden, you!
Men! girls, like men! why, if they had been men
You need not set your thoughts in rubric thus
For wholesale comment." Pardon, I am shamed
That I must needs repeat for my excuse
What looks so little graceful: "men" (for still
My mother went revolving on the word)
"And so they are,—very like men indeed—
And with that woman closeted for hours!"
Then came these dreadful words out one by one,
"Why—these—are—men:" I shuddered: "and you know it."
"O ask me nothing," I said: "And she knows too,
And she conceals it." So my mother clutched
The truth at once, but with no word from me;
And now thus early risen she goes to inform
The Princess: Lady Psyche will be crushed;
But you may yet be saved, and therefore fly;
But heal me with your pardon ere you go.'

'What pardon, sweet Melissa, for a blush?'
Said Cyril: 'Pale one, blush again: than wear
Those lilies, better blush our lives away.
Yet let us breathe for one hour more in Heaven'

He added, 'lest some classic Angel speak
In scorn of us, "They mounted, Ganymedes,
To tumble, Vulcans, on the second morn."
But I will melt this marble into wax
To yield us farther furlough:' and he went.

Melissa shook her doubtful curls, and thought
He scarce would prosper. 'Tell us,' Florian asked,
'How grew this feud betwixt the right and left.'
'O long ago,' she said, 'betwixt these two
Division smoulders hidden; 'tis my mother,
Too jealous, often fretful as the wind
Pent in a crevice: much I bear with her:
I never knew my father, but she says
(God help her) she was wedded to a fool;
And still she railed against the state of things.
She had the care of Lady Ida's youth,
And from the Queen's decease she brought her up.
But when your sister came she won the heart
Of Ida: they were still together, grew
(For so they said themselves) inosculated;
Consonant chords that shiver to one note;
One mind in all things: yet my mother still
Affirms your Psyche thieved her theories,
And angled with them for her pupil's love:
She calls her plagiarist; I know not what:
But I must go: I dare not tarry,' and light,
As flies the shadow of a bird, she fled.

Then murmured Florian gazing after her,
'An open-hearted maiden, true and pure.
If I could love, why this were she: how pretty
Her blushing was, and how she blushed again,
As if to close with Cyril's random wish:
Not like your Princess crammed with erring pride,
Nor like poor Psyche whom she drags in tow.'

'The crane,' I said, 'may chatter of the crane,
The dove may murmur of the dove, but I
An eagle clang an eagle to the sphere.
My princess, O my princess! true she errs,
But in her own grand way: being herself
Three times more noble than three score of men,
She sees herself in every woman else,
And so she wears her error like a crown
To blind the truth and me: for her, and her,
Hebes are they to hand ambrosia, mix
The nectar; but—ah she—whene'er she moves
The Samian Herè rises and she speaks
A Memnon smitten with the morning Sun.'

So saying from the court we paced, and gained
The terrace ranged along the Northern front,
And leaning there on those balusters, high
Above the empurpled champaign, drank the gale
That blown about the foliage underneath,
And sated with the innumerable rose,
Beat balm upon our eyelids. Hither came

Cyril, and yawning 'O hard task,' he cried;

'No fighting shadows here! I forced a way

Through opposition crabbed and gnarled.

Better to clear prime forests, heave and thump

A league of street in summer solstice down,

Than hammer at this reverend gentlewoman.

I knocked and, bidden, entered; found her there

At point to move, and settled in her eyes

The green malignant light of coming storm.

Sir, I was courteous, every phrase well-oiled,

As man's could be; yet maiden-meek I prayed

Concealment: she demanded who we were,

And why we came? I fabled nothing fair,

But, your example pilot, told her all.

Up went the hushed amaze of hand and eye.

But when I dwelt upon your old affiance,

She answered sharply that I talked astray.

I urged the fierce inscription on the gate,

And our three lives. True—we had limed ourselves

With open eyes, and we must take the chance.

But such extremes, I told her, well might harm

The woman's cause. "Not more than now," she said,

"So puddled as it is with favouritism."

I tried the mother's heart. Shame might befall

Melissa, knowing, saying not she knew:

Her answer was "Leave me to deal with that."

I spoke of war to come and many deaths,

And she replied, her duty was to speak,

And duty duty, clear of consequences.

I grew discouraged, Sir; but since I knew
No rock so hard but that a little wave
May beat admission in a thousand years,
I recommenced; "Decide not ere you pause.
I find you here but in the second place,
Some say the third—the authentic foundress you.
I offer boldly: we will seat you highest:
Wink at our advent: help my prince to gain
His rightful bride, and here I promise you
Some palace in our land, where you shall reign
The head and heart of all our fair she-world,
And your great name flow on with broadening time
For ever." Well, she balanced this a little,
And told me she would answer us today,
meantime be mute: thus much, nor more I gained.'

He ceasing, came a message from the Head.
'That afternoon the Princess rode to take
The dip of certain strata to the North.
Would we go with her? we should find the land
Worth seeing; and the river made a fall
Out yonder:' then she pointed on to where
A double hill ran up his furrowy forks
Beyond the thick-leaved platans of the vale.

Agreed to, this, the day fled on through all
Its range of duties to the appointed hour.
Then summoned to the porch we went. She stood
Among her maidens, higher by the head,

Her back against a pillar, her foot on one
Of those tame leopards. Kittenlike he rolled
And pawed about her sandal. I drew near;
I gazed. On a sudden my strange seizure came
Upon me, the weird vision of our house:
The Princess Ida seemed a hollow show,
Her gay-furred cats a painted fantasy,
Her college and her maidens, empty masks,
And I myself the shadow of a dream,
For all things were and were not. Yet I felt
My heart beat thick with passion and with awe;
Then from my breast the involuntary sigh
Brake, as she smote me with the light of eyes
That lent my knee desire to kneel, and shook
My pulses, till to horse we got, and so
Went forth in long retinue following up
The river as it narrowed to the hills.

I rode beside her and to me she said:
'O friend, we trust that you esteemed us not
Too harsh to your companion yestermorn;
Unwillingly we spake.' 'No—not to her,'
I answered, 'but to one of whom we spake
Your Highness might have seemed the thing you say.'
'Again?' she cried, 'are you ambassadresses
From him to me? we give you, being strange,
A license: speak, and let the topic die.'

I stammered that I knew him—could have wished—

'Our king expects—was there no precontract?
There is no truer-hearted—ah, you seem
　　All he prefigured, and he could not see
　　The bird of passage flying south but longed
　　To follow: surely, if your Highness keep
Your purport, you will shock him even to death,
　　Or baser courses, children of despair.'

'Poor boy,' she said, 'can he not read—no books?
Quoit, tennis, ball—no games? nor deals in that
　　Which men delight in, martial exercise?
　　To nurse a blind ideal like a girl,
　　Methinks he seems no better than a girl;
As girls were once, as we ourself have been:
We had our dreams; perhaps he mixt with them:
We touch on our dead self, nor shun to do it,
Being other—since we learnt our meaning here,
　　To lift the woman's fallen divinity
　　Upon an even pedestal with man.'

She paused, and added with a haughtier smile
　'And as to precontracts, we move, my friend,
At no man's beck, but know ourself and thee,
　　O Vashti, noble Vashti! Summoned out
　　She kept her state, and left the drunken king
　　To brawl at Shushan underneath the palms.'

'Alas your Highness breathes full East,' I said,
'On that which leans to you. I know the Prince,

I prize his truth: and then how vast a work
To assail this gray preëminence of man!
You grant me license; might I use it? think;
Ere half be done perchance your life may fail;
Then comes the feebler heiress of your plan,
And takes and ruins all; and thus your pains
May only make that footprint upon sand
Which old-recurring waves of prejudice
Resmooth to nothing: might I dread that you,
With only Fame for spouse and your great deeds
For issue, yet may live in vain, and miss,
Meanwhile, what every woman counts her due,
Love, children, happiness?'

And she exclaimed,
'Peace, you young savage of the Northern wild!
What! though your Prince's love were like a God's,
Have we not made ourself the sacrifice?
You are bold indeed: we are not talked to thus:
Yet will we say for children, would they grew
Like field-flowers everywhere! we like them well:
But children die; and let me tell you, girl,
Howe'er you babble, great deeds cannot die;
They with the sun and moon renew their light
For ever, blessing those that look on them.
Children—that men may pluck them from our hearts,
Kill us with pity, break us with ourselves—
O—children—there is nothing upon earth
More miserable than she that has a son
And sees him err: nor would we work for fame;

Though she perhaps might reap the applause of Great,
Who earns the one POU STO whence after-hands
May move the world, though she herself effect
But little: wherefore up and act, nor shrink
For fear our solid aim be dissipated
By frail successors. Would, indeed, we had been,
In lieu of many mortal flies, a race
Of giants living, each, a thousand years,
That we might see our own work out, and watch
The sandy footprint harden into stone.'

I answered nothing, doubtful in myself
If that strange Poet-princess with her grand
Imaginations might at all be won.
And she broke out interpreting my thoughts:

'No doubt we seem a kind of monster to you;
We are used to that: for women, up till this
Cramped under worse than South-sea-isle taboo,
Dwarfs of the gynæceum, fail so far
In high desire, they know not, cannot guess
How much their welfare is a passion to us.
If we could give them surer, quicker proof—
Oh if our end were less achievable
By slow approaches, than by single act
Of immolation, any phase of death,
We were as prompt to spring against the pikes,
Or down the fiery gulf as talk of it,
To compass our dear sisters' liberties.'

She bowed as if to veil a noble tear;
And up we came to where the river sloped
To plunge in cataract, shattering on black blocks
A breadth of thunder. O'er it shook the woods,
And danced the colour, and, below, stuck out
The bones of some vast bulk that lived and roared
Before man was. She gazed awhile and said,
'As these rude bones to us, are we to her
That will be.' 'Dare we dream of that,' I asked,
'Which wrought us, as the workman and his work,
That practice betters?' 'How,' she cried, 'you love
The metaphysics! read and earn our prize,
A golden brooch: beneath an emerald plane
Sits Diotima, teaching him that died
Of hemlock; our device; wrought to the life;
She rapt upon her subject, he on her:
For there are schools for all.' 'And yet' I said
'Methinks I have not found among them all
One anatomic.' 'Nay, we thought of that,'
She answered, 'but it pleased us not: in truth
We shudder but to dream our maids should ape
Those monstrous males that carve the living hound,
And cram him with the fragments of the grave,
Or in the dark dissolving human heart,
And holy secrets of this microcosm,
Dabbling a shameless hand with shameful jest,
Encarnalize their spirits: yet we know
Knowledge is knowledge, and this matter hangs:

Howbeit ourself, foreseeing casualty,

Nor willing men should come among us, learnt,

For many weary moons before we came,

This craft of healing. Were you sick, ourself

Would tend upon you. To your question now,

Which touches on the workman and his work.

Let there be light and there was light: 'tis so:

For was, and is, and will be, are but is;

And all creation is one act at once,

The birth of light: but we that are not all,

As parts, can see but parts, now this, now that,

And live, perforce, from thought to thought, and make

One act a phantom of succession: thus

Our weakness somehow shapes the shadow, Time;

But in the shadow will we work, and mould

The woman to the fuller day.'

She spake

With kindled eyes; we rode a league beyond,

And, o'er a bridge of pinewood crossing, came

On flowery levels underneath the crag,

Full of all beauty. 'O how sweet' I said

(For I was half-oblivious of my mask)

'To linger here with one that loved us.' 'Yea,'

She answered, 'or with fair philosophies

That lift the fancy; for indeed these fields

Are lovely, lovelier not the Elysian lawns,

Where paced the Demigods of old, and saw

The soft white vapour streak the crownèd towers

Built to the Sun:' then, turning to her maids,

'Pitch our pavilion here upon the sward;
Lay out the viands.' At the word, they raised
A tent of satin, elaborately wrought
With fair Corinna's triumph; here she stood,
Engirt with many a florid maiden-cheek,
The woman-conqueror; woman-conquered there
The bearded Victor of ten-thousand hymns,
And all the men mourned at his side: but we
Set forth to climb; then, climbing, Cyril kept
With Psyche, with Melissa Florian, I
With mine affianced. Many a little hand
Glanced like a touch of sunshine on the rocks,
Many a light foot shone like a jewel set
In the dark crag: and then we turned, we wound
About the cliffs, the copses, out and in,
Hammering and clinking, chattering stony names
Of shales and hornblende, rag and trap and tuff,
Amygdaloid and trachyte, till the Sun
Grew broader toward his death and fell, and all
The rosy heights came out above the lawns.
The splendour falls on castle walls
And snowy summits old in story:
The long light shakes across the lakes,
And the wild cataract leaps in glory.
Blow, bugle, blow, set the wild echoes flying,
Blow, bugle; answer, echoes, dying, dying, dying.

O hark, O hear! how thin and clear,
And thinner, clearer, farther going!

O sweet and far from cliff and scar
The horns of Elfland faintly blowing!
Blow, let us hear the purple glens replying:
Blow, bugle; answer, echoes, dying, dying, dying.

O love, they die in yon rich sky,
They faint on hill or field or river:
Our echoes roll from soul to soul,
And grow for ever and for ever.
Blow, bugle, blow, set the wild echoes flying,
And answer, echoes, answer, dying, dying, dying.

IV

'There sinks the nebulous star we call the Sun,
If that hypothesis of theirs be sound'
Said Ida; 'let us down and rest;' and we
Down from the lean and wrinkled precipices,
By every coppice-feathered chasm and cleft,
Dropt through the ambrosial gloom to where below
No bigger than a glow-worm shone the tent
Lamp-lit from the inner. Once she leaned on me,
Descending; once or twice she lent her hand,
And blissful palpitations in the blood,
Stirring a sudden transport rose and fell.

But when we planted level feet, and dipt
Beneath the satin dome and entered in,
There leaning deep in broidered down we sank
Our elbows: on a tripod in the midst
A fragrant flame rose, and before us glowed
Fruit, blossom, viand, amber wine, and gold.

Then she, 'Let some one sing to us: lightlier move
The minutes fledged with music:' and a maid,
Of those beside her, smote her harp, and sang.
'Tears, idle tears, I know not what they mean,
Tears from the depth of some divine despair
Rise in the heart, and gather to the eyes,
In looking on the happy Autumn-fields,

And thinking of the days that are no more.

'Fresh as the first beam glittering on a sail,
That brings our friends up from the underworld,
Sad as the last which reddens over one
That sinks with all we love below the verge;
So sad, so fresh, the days that are no more.

'Ah, sad and strange as in dark summer dawns
The earliest pipe of half-awakened birds
To dying ears, when unto dying eyes
The casement slowly grows a glimmering square;
So sad, so strange, the days that are no more.

'Dear as remembered kisses after death,
And sweet as those by hopeless fancy feigned
On lips that are for others; deep as love,
Deep as first love, and wild with all regret;
O Death in Life, the days that are no more.'
She ended with such passion that the tear,
She sang of, shook and fell, an erring pearl
Lost in her bosom: but with some disdain
Answered the Princess, 'If indeed there haunt
About the mouldered lodges of the Past
So sweet a voice and vague, fatal to men,
Well needs it we should cram our ears with wool
And so pace by: but thine are fancies hatched
In silken-folded idleness; nor is it
Wiser to weep a true occasion lost,

But trim our sails, and let old bygones be,
While down the streams that float us each and all
To the issue, goes, like glittering bergs of ice,
Throne after throne, and molten on the waste
Becomes a cloud: for all things serve their time
Toward that great year of equal mights and rights,
Nor would I fight with iron laws, in the end
Found golden: let the past be past; let be
Their cancelled Babels: though the rough kex break
The starred mosaic, and the beard-blown goat
Hang on the shaft, and the wild figtree split
Their monstrous idols, care not while we hear
A trumpet in the distance pealing news
Of better, and Hope, a poising eagle, burns
Above the unrisen morrow:' then to me;
'Know you no song of your own land,' she said,
'Not such as moans about the retrospect,
But deals with the other distance and the hues
Of promise; not a death's-head at the wine.'

Then I remembered one myself had made,
What time I watched the swallow winging south
From mine own land, part made long since, and part
Now while I sang, and maidenlike as far
As I could ape their treble, did I sing.
'O Swallow, Swallow, flying, flying South,
Fly to her, and fall upon her gilded eaves,
And tell her, tell her, what I tell to thee.

'O tell her, Swallow, thou that knowest each,
That bright and fierce and fickle is the South,
And dark and true and tender is the North.

'O Swallow, Swallow, if I could follow, and light
Upon her lattice, I would pipe and trill,
And cheep and twitter twenty million loves.

'O were I thou that she might take me in,
And lay me on her bosom, and her heart
Would rock the snowy cradle till I died.

'Why lingereth she to clothe her heart with love,
Delaying as the tender ash delays
To clothe herself, when all the woods are green?

'O tell her, Swallow, that thy brood is flown:
Say to her, I do but wanton in the South,
But in the North long since my nest is made.

'O tell her, brief is life but love is long,
And brief the sun of summer in the North,
And brief the moon of beauty in the South.

'O Swallow, flying from the golden woods,
Fly to her, and pipe and woo her, and make her mine,
And tell her, tell her, that I follow thee.'
I ceased, and all the ladies, each at each,
Like the Ithacensian suitors in old time,

Stared with great eyes, and laughed with alien lips,
And knew not what they meant; for still my voice
Rang false: but smiling 'Not for thee,' she said,
     'O Bulbul, any rose of Gulistan
Shall burst her veil: marsh-divers, rather, maid,
     Shall croak thee sister, or the meadow-crake
Grate her harsh kindred in the grass: and this
     A mere love-poem! O for such, my friend,
We hold them slight: they mind us of the time
When we made bricks in Egypt. Knaves are men,
     That lute and flute fantastic tenderness,
     And dress the victim to the offering up,
     And paint the gates of Hell with Paradise,
     And play the slave to gain the tyranny.
     Poor soul! I had a maid of honour once;
     She wept her true eyes blind for such a one,
     A rogue of canzonets and serenades.
I loved her. Peace be with her. She is dead.
So they blaspheme the muse! But great is song
     Used to great ends: ourself have often tried
Valkyrian hymns, or into rhythm have dashed
     The passion of the prophetess; for song
     Is duer unto freedom, force and growth
     Of spirit than to junketing and love.
Love is it? Would this same mock-love, and this
     Mock-Hymen were laid up like winter bats,
     Till all men grew to rate us at our worth,
     Not vassals to be beat, nor pretty babes
To be dandled, no, but living wills, and sphered

Whole in ourselves and owed to none. Enough!
But now to leaven play with profit, you,
Know you no song, the true growth of your soil,
That gives the manners of your country-women?'

She spoke and turned her sumptuous head with eyes
Of shining expectation fixt on mine.
Then while I dragged my brains for such a song,
Cyril, with whom the bell-mouthed glass had wrought,
Or mastered by the sense of sport, began
To troll a careless, careless tavern-catch
Of Moll and Meg, and strange experiences
Unmeet for ladies. Florian nodded at him,
I frowning; Psyche flushed and wanned and shook;
The lilylike Melissa drooped her brows;
'Forbear,' the Princess cried; 'Forbear, Sir' I;
And heated through and through with wrath and love,
I smote him on the breast; he started up;
There rose a shriek as of a city sacked;
Melissa clamoured 'Flee the death;' 'To horse'
Said Ida; 'home! to horse!' and fled, as flies
A troop of snowy doves athwart the dusk,
When some one batters at the dovecote-doors,
Disorderly the women. Alone I stood
With Florian, cursing Cyril, vext at heart,
In the pavilion: there like parting hopes
I heard them passing from me: hoof by hoof,
And every hoof a knell to my desires,
Clanged on the bridge; and then another shriek,

'The Head, the Head, the Princess, O the Head!'
For blind with rage she missed the plank, and rolled
In the river. Out I sprang from glow to gloom:
There whirled her white robe like a blossomed branch
Rapt to the horrible fall: a glance I gave,
No more; but woman-vested as I was
Plunged; and the flood drew; yet I caught her; then
Oaring one arm, and bearing in my left
The weight of all the hopes of half the world,
Strove to buffet to land in vain. A tree
Was half-disrooted from his place and stooped
To wrench his dark locks in the gurgling wave
Mid-channel. Right on this we drove and caught,
And grasping down the boughs I gained the shore.

There stood her maidens glimmeringly grouped
In the hollow bank. One reaching forward drew
My burthen from mine arms; they cried 'she lives:'
They bore her back into the tent: but I,
So much a kind of shame within me wrought,
Not yet endured to meet her opening eyes,
Nor found my friends; but pushed alone on foot
(For since her horse was lost I left her mine)
Across the woods, and less from Indian craft
Than beelike instinct hiveward, found at length
The garden portals. Two great statues, Art
And Science, Caryatids, lifted up
A weight of emblem, and betwixt were valves
Of open-work in which the hunter rued

His rash intrusion, manlike, but his brows
Had sprouted, and the branches thereupon
Spread out at top, and grimly spiked the gates.

A little space was left between the horns,
Through which I clambered o'er at top with pain,
Dropt on the sward, and up the linden walks,
And, tost on thoughts that changed from hue to hue,
Now poring on the glowworm, now the star,
I paced the terrace, till the Bear had wheeled
Through a great arc his seven slow suns.
        A step
Of lightest echo, then a loftier form
Than female, moving through the uncertain gloom,
Disturbed me with the doubt 'if this were she,'
But it was Florian. 'Hist O Hist,' he said,
'They seek us: out so late is out of rules.
Moreover "seize the strangers" is the cry.
How came you here?' I told him: 'I' said he,
'Last of the train, a moral leper, I,
To whom none spake, half-sick at heart, returned.
Arriving all confused among the rest
With hooded brows I crept into the hall,
And, couched behind a Judith, underneath
The head of Holofernes peeped and saw.
Girl after girl was called to trial: each
Disclaimed all knowledge of us: last of all,
Melissa: trust me, Sir, I pitied her.
She, questioned if she knew us men, at first

Was silent; closer prest, denied it not:
And then, demanded if her mother knew,
Or Psyche, she affirmed not, or denied:
From whence the Royal mind, familiar with her,
Easily gathered either guilt. She sent
For Psyche, but she was not there; she called
For Psyche's child to cast it from the doors;
She sent for Blanche to accuse her face to face;
And I slipt out: but whither will you now?
And where are Psyche, Cyril? both are fled:
What, if together? that were not so well.
Would rather we had never come! I dread
His wildness, and the chances of the dark.'

'And yet,' I said, 'you wrong him more than I
That struck him: this is proper to the clown,
Though smocked, or furred and purpled, still the clown,
To harm the thing that trusts him, and to shame
That which he says he loves: for Cyril, howe'er
He deal in frolic, as tonight—the song
Might have been worse and sinned in grosser lips
Beyond all pardon—as it is, I hold
These flashes on the surface are not he.
He has a solid base of temperament:
But as the waterlily starts and slides
Upon the level in little puffs of wind,
Though anchored to the bottom, such is he.'

Scarce had I ceased when from a tamarisk near

Two Proctors leapt upon us, crying, 'Names:'
He, standing still, was clutched; but I began
To thrid the musky-circled mazes, wind
And double in and out the boles, and race
By all the fountains: fleet I was of foot:
Before me showered the rose in flakes; behind
I heard the puffed pursuer; at mine ear
Bubbled the nightingale and heeded not,
And secret laughter tickled all my soul.
At last I hooked my ankle in a vine,
That claspt the feet of a Mnemosyne,
And falling on my face was caught and known.

They haled us to the Princess where she sat
High in the hall: above her drooped a lamp,
And made the single jewel on her brow
Burn like the mystic fire on a mast-head,
Prophet of storm: a handmaid on each side
Bowed toward her, combing out her long black hair
Damp from the river; and close behind her stood
Eight daughters of the plough, stronger than men,
Huge women blowzed with health, and wind, and rain,
And labour. Each was like a Druid rock;
Or like a spire of land that stands apart
Cleft from the main, and wailed about with mews.

Then, as we came, the crowd dividing clove
An advent to the throne: and therebeside,
Half-naked as if caught at once from bed

And tumbled on the purple footcloth, lay
The lily-shining child; and on the left,
Bowed on her palms and folded up from wrong,
Her round white shoulder shaken with her sobs,
Melissa knelt; but Lady Blanche erect
Stood up and spake, an affluent orator.

'It was not thus, O Princess, in old days:
You prized my counsel, lived upon my lips:
I led you then to all the Castalies;
I fed you with the milk of every Muse;
I loved you like this kneeler, and you me
Your second mother: those were gracious times.
Then came your new friend: you began to change—
I saw it and grieved—to slacken and to cool;
Till taken with her seeming openness
You turned your warmer currents all to her,
To me you froze: this was my meed for all.
Yet I bore up in part from ancient love,
And partly that I hoped to win you back,
And partly conscious of my own deserts,
And partly that you were my civil head,
And chiefly you were born for something great,
In which I might your fellow-worker be,
When time should serve; and thus a noble scheme
Grew up from seed we two long since had sown;
In us true growth, in her a Jonah's gourd,
Up in one night and due to sudden sun:
We took this palace; but even from the first

You stood in your own light and darkened mine.
What student came but that you planed her path
To Lady Psyche, younger, not so wise,
A foreigner, and I your countrywoman,
I your old friend and tried, she new in all?
But still her lists were swelled and mine were lean;
Yet I bore up in hope she would be known:
Then came these wolves: they knew her: they endured,
Long-closeted with her the yestermorn,
To tell her what they were, and she to hear:
And me none told: not less to an eye like mine
A lidless watcher of the public weal,
Last night, their mask was patent, and my foot
Was to you: but I thought again: I feared
To meet a cold "We thank you, we shall hear of it
From Lady Psyche:" you had gone to her,
She told, perforce; and winning easy grace
No doubt, for slight delay, remained among us
In our young nursery still unknown, the stem
Less grain than touchwood, while my honest heat
Were all miscounted as malignant haste
To push my rival out of place and power.
But public use required she should be known;
And since my oath was ta'en for public use,
I broke the letter of it to keep the sense.
I spoke not then at first, but watched them well,
Saw that they kept apart, no mischief done;
And yet this day (though you should hate me for it)
I came to tell you; found that you had gone,

Ridden to the hills, she likewise: now, I thought,
That surely she will speak; if not, then I:
Did she? These monsters blazoned what they were,
According to the coarseness of their kind,
For thus I hear; and known at last (my work)
And full of cowardice and guilty shame,
I grant in her some sense of shame, she flies;
And I remain on whom to wreak your rage,
I, that have lent my life to build up yours,
I that have wasted here health, wealth, and time,
And talent, I—you know it—I will not boast:
Dismiss me, and I prophesy your plan,
Divorced from my experience, will be chaff
For every gust of chance, and men will say
We did not know the real light, but chased
The wisp that flickers where no foot can tread.'

She ceased: the Princess answered coldly, 'Good:
Your oath is broken: we dismiss you: go.
For this lost lamb (she pointed to the child)
Our mind is changed: we take it to ourself.'

Thereat the Lady stretched a vulture throat,
And shot from crooked lips a haggard smile.
'The plan was mine. I built the nest' she said
'To hatch the cuckoo. Rise!' and stooped to updrag
Melissa: she, half on her mother propt,
Half-drooping from her, turned her face, and cast
A liquid look on Ida, full of prayer,

Which melted Florian's fancy as she hung,

A Niobëan daughter, one arm out,

Appealing to the bolts of Heaven; and while

We gazed upon her came a little stir

About the doors, and on a sudden rushed

Among us, out of breath as one pursued,

A woman-post in flying raiment. Fear

Stared in her eyes, and chalked her face, and winged

Her transit to the throne, whereby she fell

Delivering sealed dispatches which the Head

Took half-amazed, and in her lion's mood

Tore open, silent we with blind surmise

Regarding, while she read, till over brow

And cheek and bosom brake the wrathful bloom

As of some fire against a stormy cloud,

When the wild peasant rights himself, the rick

Flames, and his anger reddens in the heavens;

For anger most it seemed, while now her breast,

Beaten with some great passion at her heart,

Palpitated, her hand shook, and we heard

In the dead hush the papers that she held

Rustle: at once the lost lamb at her feet

Sent out a bitter bleating for its dam;

The plaintive cry jarred on her ire; she crushed

The scrolls together, made a sudden turn

As if to speak, but, utterance failing her,

She whirled them on to me, as who should say

'Read,' and I read—two letters—one her sire's.

'Fair daughter, when we sent the Prince your way,
We knew not your ungracious laws, which learnt,
We, conscious of what temper you are built,
Came all in haste to hinder wrong, but fell
Into his father's hands, who has this night,
You lying close upon his territory,
Slipt round and in the dark invested you,
And here he keeps me hostage for his son.'

The second was my father's running thus:
'You have our son: touch not a hair of his head:
Render him up unscathed: give him your hand:
Cleave to your contract: though indeed we hear
You hold the woman is the better man;
A rampant heresy, such as if it spread
Would make all women kick against their Lords
Through all the world, and which might well deserve
That we this night should pluck your palace down;
And we will do it, unless you send us back
Our son, on the instant, whole.'
So far I read;
And then stood up and spoke impetuously.

'O not to pry and peer on your reserve,
But led by golden wishes, and a hope
The child of regal compact, did I break
Your precinct; not a scorner of your sex
But venerator, zealous it should be
All that it might be: hear me, for I bear,

Though man, yet human, whatsoe'er your wrongs,

From the flaxen curl to the gray lock a life

Less mine than yours: my nurse would tell me of you;

I babbled for you, as babies for the moon,

Vague brightness; when a boy, you stooped to me

From all high places, lived in all fair lights,

Came in long breezes rapt from inmost south

And blown to inmost north; at eve and dawn

With Ida, Ida, Ida, rang the woods;

The leader wildswan in among the stars

Would clang it, and lapt in wreaths of glowworm light

The mellow breaker murmured Ida. Now,

Because I would have reached you, had you been

Sphered up with Cassiopëia, or the enthroned

Persephonè in Hades, now at length,

Those winters of abeyance all worn out,

A man I came to see you: but indeed,

Not in this frequence can I lend full tongue,

O noble Ida, to those thoughts that wait

On you, their centre: let me say but this,

That many a famous man and woman, town

And landskip, have I heard of, after seen

The dwarfs of presage: though when known, there grew

Another kind of beauty in detail

Made them worth knowing; but in you I found

My boyish dream involved and dazzled down

And mastered, while that after-beauty makes

Such head from act to act, from hour to hour,

Within me, that except you slay me here,

According to your bitter statute-book,
I cannot cease to follow you, as they say
The seal does music; who desire you more
Than growing boys their manhood; dying lips,
With many thousand matters left to do,
The breath of life; O more than poor men wealth,
Than sick men health—yours, yours, not mine—but half
Without you; with you, whole; and of those halves
You worthiest; and howe'er you block and bar
Your heart with system out from mine, I hold
That it becomes no man to nurse despair,
But in the teeth of clenched antagonisms
To follow up the worthiest till he die:
Yet that I came not all unauthorized
Behold your father's letter.'
On one knee
Kneeling, I gave it, which she caught, and dashed
Unopened at her feet: a tide of fierce
Invective seemed to wait behind her lips,
As waits a river level with the dam
Ready to burst and flood the world with foam:
And so she would have spoken, but there rose
A hubbub in the court of half the maids
Gathered together: from the illumined hall
Long lanes of splendour slanted o'er a press
Of snowy shoulders, thick as herded ewes,
And rainbow robes, and gems and gemlike eyes,
And gold and golden heads; they to and fro
Fluctuated, as flowers in storm, some red, some pale,

All open-mouthed, all gazing to the light,
Some crying there was an army in the land,
And some that men were in the very walls,
And some they cared not; till a clamour grew
As of a new-world Babel, woman-built,
And worse-confounded: high above them stood
The placid marble Muses, looking peace.

Not peace she looked, the Head: but rising up
Robed in the long night of her deep hair, so
To the open window moved, remaining there
Fixt like a beacon-tower above the waves
Of tempest, when the crimson-rolling eye
Glares ruin, and the wild birds on the light
Dash themselves dead. She stretched her arms and called
Across the tumult and the tumult fell.

'What fear ye, brawlers? am not I your Head?
On me, me, me, the storm first breaks: I dare
All these male thunderbolts: what is it ye fear?
Peace! there are those to avenge us and they come:
If not,—myself were like enough, O girls,
To unfurl the maiden banner of our rights,
And clad in iron burst the ranks of war,
Or, falling, promartyr of our cause,
Die: yet I blame you not so much for fear:
Six thousand years of fear have made you that
From which I would redeem you: but for those
That stir this hubbub—you and you—I know

Your faces there in the crowd—tomorrow morn
We hold a great convention: then shall they
That love their voices more than duty, learn
With whom they deal, dismissed in shame to live
No wiser than their mothers, household stuff,
Live chattels, mincers of each other's fame,
Full of weak poison, turnspits for the clown,
The drunkard's football, laughing-stocks of Time,
Whose brains are in their hands and in their heels
But fit to flaunt, to dress, to dance, to thrum,
To tramp, to scream, to burnish, and to scour,
For ever slaves at home and fools abroad.'

She, ending, waved her hands: thereat the crowd
Muttering, dissolved: then with a smile, that looked
A stroke of cruel sunshine on the cliff,
When all the glens are drowned in azure gloom
Of thunder-shower, she floated to us and said:

'You have done well and like a gentleman,
And like a prince: you have our thanks for all:
And you look well too in your woman's dress:
Well have you done and like a gentleman.
You saved our life: we owe you bitter thanks:
Better have died and spilt our bones in the flood—
Then men had said—but now—What hinders me
To take such bloody vengeance on you both?—
Yet since our father—Wasps in our good hive,
You would-be quenchers of the light to be,

Barbarians, grosser than your native bears—
O would I had his sceptre for one hour!
You that have dared to break our bound, and gulled
Our servants, wronged and lied and thwarted us—
I wed with thee! I bound by precontract
Your bride, your bondslave! not though all the gold
That veins the world were packed to make your crown,
And every spoken tongue should lord you. Sir,
Your falsehood and yourself are hateful to us:
I trample on your offers and on you:
Begone: we will not look upon you more.
Here, push them out at gates.'
In wrath she spake.
Then those eight mighty daughters of the plough
Bent their broad faces toward us and addressed
Their motion: twice I sought to plead my cause,
But on my shoulder hung their heavy hands,
The weight of destiny: so from her face
They pushed us, down the steps, and through the court,
And with grim laughter thrust us out at gates.

We crossed the street and gained a petty mound
Beyond it, whence we saw the lights and heard the voices murmuring.
While I listened, came
On a sudden the weird seizure and the doubt:
I seemed to move among a world of ghosts;
The Princess with her monstrous woman-guard,
The jest and earnest working side by side,
The cataract and the tumult and the kings

Were shadows; and the long fantastic night
With all its doings had and had not been,
And all things were and were not.
This went by
As strangely as it came, and on my spirits
Settled a gentle cloud of melancholy;
Not long; I shook it off; for spite of doubts
And sudden ghostly shadowings I was one
To whom the touch of all mischance but came
As night to him that sitting on a hill
Sees the midsummer, midnight, Norway sun
Set into sunrise; then we moved away.
Thy voice is heard through rolling drums,
That beat to battle where he stands;
Thy face across his fancy comes,
And gives the battle to his hands:
A moment, while the trumpets blow,
He sees his brood about thy knee;
The next, like fire he meets the foe,
And strikes him dead for thine and thee.
So Lilia sang: we thought her half-possessed,
She struck such warbling fury through the words;
And, after, feigning pique at what she called
The raillery, or grotesque, or false sublime—
Like one that wishes at a dance to change
The music—clapt her hands and cried for war,
Or some grand fight to kill and make an end:
And he that next inherited the tale
Half turning to the broken statue, said,

'Sir Ralph has got your colours: if I prove
Your knight, and fight your battle, what for me?'
It chanced, her empty glove upon the tomb
Lay by her like a model of her hand.
She took it and she flung it. 'Fight' she said,
'And make us all we would be, great and good.'
He knightlike in his cap instead of casque,
A cap of Tyrol borrowed from the hall,
Arranged the favour, and assumed the Prince.

V

Now, scarce three paces measured from the mound,
We stumbled on a stationary voice,
And 'Stand, who goes?' 'Two from the palace' I.
'The second two: they wait,' he said, 'pass on;
His Highness wakes:' and one, that clashed in arms,
By glimmering lanes and walls of canvas led
Threading the soldier-city, till we heard
The drowsy folds of our great ensign shake
From blazoned lions o'er the imperial tent
Whispers of war.
Entering, the sudden light
Dazed me half-blind: I stood and seemed to hear,
As in a poplar grove when a light wind wakes
A lisping of the innumerous leaf and dies,
Each hissing in his neighbour's ear; and then
A strangled titter, out of which there brake
On all sides, clamouring etiquette to death,
Unmeasured mirth; while now the two old kings
Began to wag their baldness up and down,
The fresh young captains flashed their glittering teeth,
The huge bush-bearded Barons heaved and blew,
And slain with laughter rolled the gilded Squire.

At length my Sire, his rough cheek wet with tears,
Panted from weary sides 'King, you are free!
We did but keep you surety for our son,

If this be he,—or a dragged mawkin, thou,
That tends to her bristled grunters in the sludge:'
For I was drenched with ooze, and torn with briers,
More crumpled than a poppy from the sheath,
And all one rag, disprinced from head to heel.
Then some one sent beneath his vaulted palm
A whispered jest to some one near him, 'Look,
He has been among his shadows.' 'Satan take
The old women and their shadows! (thus the King
Roared) make yourself a man to fight with men.
Go: Cyril told us all.'
As boys that slink
From ferule and the trespass-chiding eye,
Away we stole, and transient in a trice
From what was left of faded woman-slough
To sheathing splendours and the golden scale
Of harness, issued in the sun, that now
Leapt from the dewy shoulders of the Earth,
And hit the Northern hills. Here Cyril met us.
A little shy at first, but by and by
We twain, with mutual pardon asked and given
For stroke and song, resoldered peace, whereon
Followed his tale. Amazed he fled away
Through the dark land, and later in the night
Had come on Psyche weeping: 'then we fell
Into your father's hand, and there she lies,
But will not speak, or stir.'
He showed a tent
A stone-shot off: we entered in, and there

Among piled arms and rough accoutrements,
  Pitiful sight, wrapped in a soldier's cloak,
Like some sweet sculpture draped from head to foot,
  And pushed by rude hands from its pedestal,
  All her fair length upon the ground she lay:
  And at her head a follower of the camp,
  A charred and wrinkled piece of womanhood,
  Sat watching like the watcher by the dead.

Then Florian knelt, and 'Come' he whispered to her,
  'Lift up your head, sweet sister: lie not thus.
What have you done but right? you could not slay
  Me, nor your prince: look up: be comforted:
  Sweet is it to have done the thing one ought,
  When fallen in darker ways.' And likewise I:
  'Be comforted: have I not lost her too,
  In whose least act abides the nameless charm
That none has else for me?' She heard, she moved,
  She moaned, a folded voice; and up she sat,
And raised the cloak from brows as pale and smooth
  As those that mourn half-shrouded over death
In deathless marble. 'Her,' she said, 'my friend—
  Parted from her—betrayed her cause and mine—
Where shall I breathe? why kept ye not your faith?
  O base and bad! what comfort? none for me!'
  To whom remorseful Cyril, 'Yet I pray
  Take comfort: live, dear lady, for your child!'
  At which she lifted up her voice and cried.

'Ah me, my babe, my blossom, ah, my child,

My one sweet child, whom I shall see no more!

For now will cruel Ida keep her back;

And either she will die from want of care,

Or sicken with ill-usage, when they say

The child is hers—for every little fault,

The child is hers; and they will beat my girl

Remembering her mother: O my flower!

Or they will take her, they will make her hard,

And she will pass me by in after-life

With some cold reverence worse than were she dead.

Ill mother that I was to leave her there,

To lag behind, scared by the cry they made,

The horror of the shame among them all:

But I will go and sit beside the doors,

And make a wild petition night and day,

Until they hate to hear me like a wind

Wailing for ever, till they open to me,

And lay my little blossom at my feet,

My babe, my sweet Aglaïa, my one child:

And I will take her up and go my way,

And satisfy my soul with kissing her:

Ah! what might that man not deserve of me

Who gave me back my child?' 'Be comforted,'

Said Cyril, 'you shall have it:' but again

She veiled her brows, and prone she sank, and so

Like tender things that being caught feign death,

Spoke not, nor stirred.

By this a murmur ran

Through all the camp and inward raced the scouts
With rumour of Prince Arab hard at hand.
We left her by the woman, and without
Found the gray kings at parle: and 'Look you' cried
My father 'that our compact be fulfilled:
You have spoilt this child; she laughs at you and man:
She wrongs herself, her sex, and me, and him:
But red-faced war has rods of steel and fire;
She yields, or war.'
Then Gama turned to me:
'We fear, indeed, you spent a stormy time
With our strange girl: and yet they say that still
You love her. Give us, then, your mind at large:
How say you, war or not?'
'Not war, if possible,
O king,' I said, 'lest from the abuse of war,
The desecrated shrine, the trampled year,
The smouldering homestead, and the household flower
Torn from the lintel—all the common wrong—
A smoke go up through which I loom to her
Three times a monster: now she lightens scorn
At him that mars her plan, but then would hate
(And every voice she talked with ratify it,
And every face she looked on justify it)
The general foe. More soluble is this knot,
By gentleness than war. I want her love.
What were I nigher this although we dashed
Your cities into shards with catapults,
She would not love;—or brought her chained, a slave,

The *lifting of whose eyelash is my lord,*
Not ever would she love; but brooding turn
The book of scorn, till all my flitting chance
Were caught within the record of her wrongs,
And crushed to death: and rather, Sire, than this
I would the old God of war himself were dead,
Forgotten, rusting on his iron hills,
Rotting on some wild shore with ribs of wreck,
Or like an old-world mammoth bulked in ice,
Not to be molten out.'
And roughly spake
My father, 'Tut, you know them not, the girls.
Boy, when I hear you prate I almost think
That idiot legend credible. Look you, Sir!
Man is the hunter; woman is his game:
The sleek and shining creatures of the chase,
We hunt them for the beauty of their skins;
They love us for it, and we ride them down.
Wheedling and siding with them! Out! for shame!
Boy, there's no rose that's half so dear to them
As he that does the thing they dare not do,
Breathing and sounding beauteous battle, comes
With the air of the trumpet round him, and leaps in
Among the women, snares them by the score
Flattered and flustered, wins, though dashed with death
He reddens what he kisses: thus I won
You mother, a good mother, a good wife,
Worth winning; but this firebrand—gentleness
To such as her! if Cyril spake her true,

To catch a dragon in a cherry net,
To trip a tigress with a gossamer
Were wisdom to it.'
'Yea but Sire,' I cried,
'Wild natures need wise curbs. The soldier? No:
What dares not Ida do that she should prize
The soldier? I beheld her, when she rose
The yesternight, and storming in extremes,
Stood for her cause, and flung defiance down
Gagelike to man, and had not shunned the death,
No, not the soldier's: yet I hold her, king,
True woman: you clash them all in one,
That have as many differences as we.
The violet varies from the lily as far
As oak from elm: one loves the soldier, one
The silken priest of peace, one this, one that,
And some unworthily; their sinless faith,
A maiden moon that sparkles on a sty,
Glorifying clown and satyr; whence they need
More breadth of culture: is not Ida right?
They worth it? truer to the law within?
Severer in the logic of a life?
Twice as magnetic to sweet influences
Of earth and heaven? and she of whom you speak,
My mother, looks as whole as some serene
Creation minted in the golden moods
Of sovereign artists; not a thought, a touch,
But pure as lines of green that streak the white
Of the first snowdrop's inner leaves; I say,

Not like the piebald miscellany, man,
Bursts of great heart and slips in sensual mire,
But whole and one: and take them all-in-all,
Were we ourselves but half as good, as kind,
As truthful, much that Ida claims as right
Had ne'er been mooted, but as frankly theirs
As dues of Nature. To our point: not war:
Lest I lose all.'
'Nay, nay, you spake but sense'
Said Gama. 'We remember love ourself
In our sweet youth; we did not rate him then
This red-hot iron to be shaped with blows.
You talk almost like Ida: she can talk;
And there is something in it as you say:
But you talk kindlier: we esteem you for it.—
He seems a gracious and a gallant Prince,
I would he had our daughter: for the rest,
Our own detention, why, the causes weighed,
Fatherly fears—you used us courteously—
We would do much to gratify your Prince—
We pardon it; and for your ingress here
Upon the skirt and fringe of our fair land,
you did but come as goblins in the night,
Nor in the furrow broke the ploughman's head,
Nor burnt the grange, nor bussed the milking-maid,
Nor robbed the farmer of his bowl of cream:
But let your Prince (our royal word upon it,
He comes back safe) ride with us to our lines,
And speak with Arac: Arac's word is thrice

As ours with Ida: something may be done—
I know not what—and ours shall see us friends.
You, likewise, our late guests, if so you will,
Follow us: who knows? we four may build some plan
Foursquare to opposition.'
Here he reached
White hands of farewell to my sire, who growled
An answer which, half-muffled in his beard,
Let so much out as gave us leave to go.

Then rode we with the old king across the lawns
Beneath huge trees, a thousand rings of Spring
In every bole, a song on every spray
Of birds that piped their Valentines, and woke
Desire in me to infuse my tale of love
In the old king's ears, who promised help, and oozed
All o'er with honeyed answer as we rode
And blossom-fragrant slipt the heavy dews
Gathered by night and peace, with each light air
On our mailed heads: but other thoughts than Peace
Burnt in us, when we saw the embattled squares,
And squadrons of the Prince, trampling the flowers
With clamour: for among them rose a cry
As if to greet the king; they made a halt;
The horses yelled; they clashed their arms; the drum
Beat; merrily-blowing shrilled the martial fife;
And in the blast and bray of the long horn
And serpent-throated bugle, undulated
The banner: anon to meet us lightly pranced

Three captains out; nor ever had I seen
Such thews of men: the midmost and the highest
Was Arac: all about his motion clung
The shadow of his sister, as the beam
Of the East, that played upon them, made them glance
Like those three stars of the airy Giant's zone,
That glitter burnished by the frosty dark;
And as the fiery Sirius alters hue,
And bickers into red and emerald, shone
Their morions, washed with morning, as they came.

And I that prated peace, when first I heard
War-music, felt the blind wildbeast of force,
Whose home is in the sinews of a man,
Stir in me as to strike: then took the king
His three broad sons; with now a wandering hand
And now a pointed finger, told them all:
A common light of smiles at our disguise
Broke from their lips, and, ere the windy jest
Had laboured down within his ample lungs,
The genial giant, Arac, rolled himself
Thrice in the saddle, then burst out in words.

'Our land invaded, 'sdeath! and he himself
Your captive, yet my father wills not war:
And, 'sdeath! myself, what care I, war or no?
but then this question of your troth remains:
And there's a downright honest meaning in her;
She flies too high, she flies too high! and yet

She asked but space and fairplay for her scheme;
She prest and prest it on me—I myself,
What know I of these things? but, life and soul!
I thought her half-right talking of her wrongs;
I say she flies too high, 'sdeath! what of that?
I take her for the flower of womankind,
And so I often told her, right or wrong,
And, Prince, she can be sweet to those she loves,
And, right or wrong, I care not: this is all,
I stand upon her side: she made me swear it—
'Sdeath—and with solemn rites by candle-light—
Swear by St something—I forget her name—
Her that talked down the fifty wisest men;
She was a princess too; and so I swore.
Come, this is all; she will not: waive your claim:
If not, the foughten field, what else, at once
Decides it, 'sdeath! against my father's will.'

I lagged in answer loth to render up
My precontract, and loth by brainless war
To cleave the rift of difference deeper yet;
Till one of those two brothers, half aside
And fingering at the hair about his lip,
To prick us on to combat 'Like to like!
The woman's garment hid the woman's heart.'
A taunt that clenched his purpose like a blow!
For fiery-short was Cyril's counter-scoff,
And sharp I answered, touched upon the point
Where idle boys are cowards to their shame,

'Decide it here: why not? we are three to three.'

Then spake the third 'But three to three? no more?
No more, and in our noble sister's cause?
More, more, for honour: every captain waits
Hungry for honour, angry for his king.
More, more some fifty on a side, that each
May breathe himself, and quick! by overthrow
Of these or those, the question settled die.'

'Yea,' answered I, 'for this wreath of air,
This flake of rainbow flying on the highest
Foam of men's deeds—this honour, if ye will.
It needs must be for honour if at all:
Since, what decision? if we fail, we fail,
And if we win, we fail: she would not keep
Her compact.' "Sdeath! but we will send to her,'
Said Arac, 'worthy reasons why she should
Bide by this issue: let our missive through,
And you shall have her answer by the word.'

'Boys!' shrieked the old king, but vainlier than a hen
To her false daughters in the pool; for none
Regarded; neither seemed there more to say:
Back rode we to my father's camp, and found
He thrice had sent a herald to the gates,
To learn if Ida yet would cede our claim,
Or by denial flush her babbling wells
With her own people's life: three times he went:

- 85 -

The first, he blew and blew, but none appeared:
He battered at the doors; none came: the next,
An awful voice within had warned him thence:
The third, and those eight daughters of the plough
Came sallying through the gates, and caught his hair,
And so belaboured him on rib and cheek
They made him wild: not less one glance he caught
Through open doors of Ida stationed there
Unshaken, clinging to her purpose, firm
Though compassed by two armies and the noise
Of arms; and standing like a stately Pine
Set in a cataract on an island-crag,
When storm is on the heights, and right and left
Sucked from the dark heart of the long hills roll
The torrents, dashed to the vale: and yet her will
Bred will in me to overcome it or fall.

But when I told the king that I was pledged
To fight in tourney for my bride, he clashed
His iron palms together with a cry;
Himself would tilt it out among the lads:
But overborne by all his bearded lords
With reasons drawn from age and state, perforce
He yielded, wroth and red, with fierce demur:
And many a bold knight started up in heat,
And sware to combat for my claim till death.

All on this side the palace ran the field
Flat to the garden-wall: and likewise here,

Above the garden's glowing blossom-belts,
A columned entry shone and marble stairs,
And great bronze valves, embossed with Tomyris
And what she did to Cyrus after fight,
But now fast barred: so here upon the flat
All that long morn the lists were hammered up,
And all that morn the heralds to and fro,
With message and defiance, went and came;
Last, Ida's answer, in a royal hand,
But shaken here and there, and rolling words
Oration-like. I kissed it and I read.

'O brother, you have known the pangs we felt,
What heats of indignation when we heard
Of those that iron-cramped their women's feet;
Of lands in which at the altar the poor bride
Gives her harsh groom for bridal-gift a scourge;
Of living hearts that crack within the fire
Where smoulder their dead despots; and of those,—
Mothers,—that, with all prophetic pity, fling
Their pretty maids in the running flood, and swoops
The vulture, beak and talon, at the heart
Made for all noble motion: and I saw
That equal baseness lived in sleeker times
With smoother men: the old leaven leavened all:
Millions of throats would bawl for civil rights,
No woman named: therefore I set my face
Against all men, and lived but for mine own.
Far off from men I built a fold for them:

I stored it full of rich memorial:
I fenced it round with gallant institutes,
And biting laws to scare the beasts of prey
And prospered; till a rout of saucy boys
Brake on us at our books, and marred our peace,
Masked like our maids, blustering I know not what
Of insolence and love, some pretext held
Of baby troth, invalid, since my will
Sealed not the bond—the striplings! for their sport!—
I tamed my leopards: shall I not tame these?
Or you? or I? for since you think me touched
In honour—what, I would not aught of false—
Is not our case pure? and whereas I know
Your prowess, Arac, and what mother's blood
You draw from, fight; you failing, I abide
What end soever: fail you will not. Still
Take not his life: he risked it for my own;
His mother lives: yet whatsoe'er you do,
Fight and fight well; strike and strike him. O dear
Brothers, the woman's Angel guards you, you
The sole men to be mingled with our cause,
The sole men we shall prize in the after-time,
Your very armour hallowed, and your statues
Reared, sung to, when, this gad-fly brushed aside,
We plant a solid foot into the Time,
And mould a generation strong to move
With claim on claim from right to right, till she
Whose name is yoked with children's, know herself;
And Knowledge in our own land make her free,

And, ever following those two crownèd twins,
Commerce and conquest, shower the fiery grain
Of freedom broadcast over all the orbs
Between the Northern and the Southern morn.'

Then came a postscript dashed across the rest.
'See that there be no traitors in your camp:
We seem a nest of traitors—none to trust
Since our arms failed—this Egypt-plague of men!
Almost our maids were better at their homes,
Than thus man-girdled here: indeed I think
Our chiefest comfort is the little child
Of one unworthy mother; which she left:
She shall not have it back: the child shall grow
To prize the authentic mother of her mind.
I took it for an hour in mine own bed
This morning: there the tender orphan hands
Felt at my heart, and seemed to charm from thence
The wrath I nursed against the world: farewell.'

I ceased; he said, 'Stubborn, but she may sit
Upon a king's right hand in thunder-storms,
And breed up warriors! See now, though yourself
Be dazzled by the wildfire Love to sloughs
That swallow common sense, the spindling king,
This Gama swamped in lazy tolerance.
When the man wants weight, the woman takes it up,
And topples down the scales; but this is fixt
As are the roots of earth and base of all;

- 89 -

Man for the field and woman for the hearth:
Man for the sword and for the needle she:
Man with the head and woman with the heart:
Man to command and woman to obey;
All else confusion. Look you! the gray mare
Is ill to live with, when her whinny shrills
From tile to scullery, and her small goodman
Shrinks in his arm-chair while the fires of Hell
Mix with his hearth: but you—she's yet a colt—
Take, break her: strongly groomed and straitly curbed
She might not rank with those detestable
That let the bantling scald at home, and brawl
Their rights and wrongs like potherbs in the street.
They say she's comely; there's the fairer chance:
I like her none the less for rating at her!
Besides, the woman wed is not as we,
But suffers change of frame. A lusty brace
Of twins may weed her of her folly. Boy,
The bearing and the training of a child
Is woman's wisdom.'
Thus the hard old king:
I took my leave, for it was nearly noon:
I pored upon her letter which I held,
And on the little clause 'take not his life:'
I mused on that wild morning in the woods,
And on the 'Follow, follow, thou shalt win:'
I thought on all the wrathful king had said,
And how the strange betrothment was to end:
Then I remembered that burnt sorcerer's curse

That one should fight with shadows and should fall;
And like a flash the weird affection came:
King, camp and college turned to hollow shows;
I seemed to move in old memorial tilts,
And doing battle with forgotten ghosts,
To dream myself the shadow of a dream:
And ere I woke it was the point of noon,
The lists were ready. Empanoplied and plumed
We entered in, and waited, fifty there
Opposed to fifty, till the trumpet blared
At the barrier like a wild horn in a land
Of echoes, and a moment, and once more
The trumpet, and again: at which the storm
Of galloping hoofs bare on the ridge of spears
And riders front to front, until they closed
In conflict with the crash of shivering points,
And thunder. Yet it seemed a dream, I dreamed
Of fighting. On his haunches rose the steed,
And into fiery splinters leapt the lance,
And out of stricken helmets sprang the fire.
Part sat like rocks: part reeled but kept their seats:
Part rolled on the earth and rose again and drew:
Part stumbled mixt with floundering horses. Down
From those two bulks at Arac's side, and down
From Arac's arm, as from a giant's flail,
The large blows rained, as here and everywhere
He rode the mellay, lord of the ringing lists,
And all the plain,—brand, mace, and shaft, and shield—
Shocked, like an iron-clanging anvil banged

With hammers; till I thought, can this be he
From Gama's dwarfish loins? if this be so,
The mother makes us most—and in my dream
I glanced aside, and saw the palace-front
Alive with fluttering scarfs and ladies' eyes,
And highest, among the statues, statuelike,
Between a cymballed Miriam and a Jael,
With Psyche's babe, was Ida watching us,
A single band of gold about her hair,
Like a Saint's glory up in heaven: but she
No saint—inexorable—no tenderness—
Too hard, too cruel: yet she sees me fight,
Yea, let her see me fall! and with that I drave
Among the thickest and bore down a Prince,
And Cyril, one. Yea, let me make my dream
All that I would. But that large-moulded man,
His visage all agrin as at a wake,
Made at me through the press, and, staggering back
With stroke on stroke the horse and horseman, came
As comes a pillar of electric cloud,
Flaying the roofs and sucking up the drains,
And shadowing down the champaign till it strikes
On a wood, and takes, and breaks, and cracks, and splits,
And twists the grain with such a roar that Earth
Reels, and the herdsmen cry; for everything
Gave way before him: only Florian, he
That loved me closer than his own right eye,
Thrust in between; but Arac rode him down:
And Cyril seeing it, pushed against the Prince,

With Psyche's colour round his helmet, tough,
Strong, supple, sinew-corded, apt at arms;
But tougher, heavier, stronger, he that smote
And threw him: last I spurred; I felt my veins
Stretch with fierce heat; a moment hand to hand,
And sword to sword, and horse to horse we hung,
Till I struck out and shouted; the blade glanced,
I did but shear a feather, and dream and truth
Flowed from me; darkness closed me; and I fell.

Home they brought her warrior dead:
She nor swooned, nor uttered cry:
All her maidens, watching, said,
'She must weep or she will die.'

Then they praised him, soft and low,
Called him worthy to be loved,
Truest friend and noblest foe;
Yet she neither spoke nor moved.

Stole a maiden from her place,
Lightly to the warrior stept,
Took the face-cloth from the face;
Yet she neither moved nor wept.

Rose a nurse of ninety years,
Set his child upon her knee—
Like summer tempest came her tears—
'Sweet my child, I live for thee.'

VI

My dream had never died or lived again.

As in some mystic middle state I lay;

Seeing I saw not, hearing not I heard:

Though, if I saw not, yet they told me all

So often that I speak as having seen.

For so it seemed, or so they said to me,

That all things grew more tragic and more strange;

That when our side was vanquished and my cause

For ever lost, there went up a great cry,

The Prince is slain. My father heard and ran

In on the lists, and there unlaced my casque

And grovelled on my body, and after him

Came Psyche, sorrowing for Aglaïa.

But high upon the palace Ida stood

With Psyche's babe in arm: there on the roofs

Like that great dame of Lapidoth she sang.

'Our enemies have fallen, have fallen: the seed,

The little seed they laughed at in the dark,

Has risen and cleft the soil, and grown a bulk

Of spanless girth, that lays on every side

A thousand arms and rushes to the Sun.

'Our enemies have fallen, have fallen: they came;

The leaves were wet with women's tears: they heard

A noise of songs they would not understand:

They marked it with the red cross to the fall,
And would have strown it, and are fallen themselves.

'Our enemies have fallen, have fallen: they came,
The woodmen with their axes: lo the tree!
But we will make it faggots for the hearth,
And shape it plank and beam for roof and floor,
And boats and bridges for the use of men.

'Our enemies have fallen, have fallen: they struck;
With their own blows they hurt themselves, nor knew
There dwelt an iron nature in the grain:
The glittering axe was broken in their arms,
Their arms were shattered to the shoulder blade.

'Our enemies have fallen, but this shall grow
A night of Summer from the heat, a breadth
Of Autumn, dropping fruits of power: and rolled
With music in the growing breeze of Time,
The tops shall strike from star to star, the fangs
Shall move the stony bases of the world.

'And now, O maids, behold our sanctuary
Is violate, our laws broken: fear we not
To break them more in their behoof, whose arms
Championed our cause and won it with a day
Blanched in our annals, and perpetual feast,
When dames and heroines of the golden year
Shall strip a hundred hollows bare of Spring,

To rain an April of ovation round
Their statues, borne aloft, the three: but come,
We will be liberal, since our rights are won.
Let them not lie in the tents with coarse mankind,
Ill nurses; but descend, and proffer these
The brethren of our blood and cause, that there
Lie bruised and maimed, the tender ministries
Of female hands and hospitality.'

She spoke, and with the babe yet in her arms,
Descending, burst the great bronze valves, and led
A hundred maids in train across the Park.
Some cowled, and some bare-headed, on they came,
Their feet in flowers, her loveliest: by them went
The enamoured air sighing, and on their curls
From the high tree the blossom wavering fell,
And over them the tremulous isles of light
Slided, they moving under shade: but Blanche
At distance followed: so they came: anon
Through open field into the lists they wound
Timorously; and as the leader of the herd
That holds a stately fretwork to the Sun,
And followed up by a hundred airy does,
Steps with a tender foot, light as on air,
The lovely, lordly creature floated on
To where her wounded brethren lay; there stayed;
Knelt on one knee,—the child on one,—and prest
Their hands, and called them dear deliverers,
And happy warriors, and immortal names,

And said 'You shall not lie in the tents but here,
And nursed by those for whom you fought, and served
With female hands and hospitality.'

Then, whether moved by this, or was it chance,
She past my way. Up started from my side
The old lion, glaring with his whelpless eye,
Silent; but when she saw me lying stark,
Dishelmed and mute, and motionlessly pale,
Cold even to her, she sighed; and when she saw
The haggard father's face and reverend beard
Of grisly twine, all dabbled with the blood
Of his own son, shuddered, a twitch of pain
Tortured her mouth, and o'er her forehead past
A shadow, and her hue changed, and she said:
'He saved my life: my brother slew him for it.'
No more: at which the king in bitter scorn
Drew from my neck the painting and the tress,
And held them up: she saw them, and a day
Rose from the distance on her memory,
When the good Queen, her mother, shore the tress
With kisses, ere the days of Lady Blanche:
And then once more she looked at my pale face:
Till understanding all the foolish work
Of Fancy, and the bitter close of all,
Her iron will was broken in her mind;
Her noble heart was molten in her breast;
She bowed, she set the child on the earth; she laid
A feeling finger on my brows, and presently

'O Sire,' she said, 'he lives: he is not dead:
O let me have him with my brethren here
In our own palace: we will tend on him
Like one of these; if so, by any means,
To lighten this great clog of thanks, that make
Our progress falter to the woman's goal.'

She said: but at the happy word 'he lives'
My father stooped, re-fathered o'er my wounds.
So those two foes above my fallen life,
With brow to brow like night and evening mixt
Their dark and gray, while Psyche ever stole
A little nearer, till the babe that by us,
Half-lapt in glowing gauze and golden brede,
Lay like a new-fallen meteor on the grass,
Uncared for, spied its mother and began
A blind and babbling laughter, and to dance
Its body, and reach its fatling innocent arms
And lazy lingering fingers. She the appeal
Brooked not, but clamouring out 'Mine—mine—not yours,
It is not yours, but mine: give me the child'
Ceased all on tremble: piteous was the cry:
So stood the unhappy mother open-mouthed,
And turned each face her way: wan was her cheek
With hollow watch, her blooming mantle torn,
Red grief and mother's hunger in her eye,
And down dead-heavy sank her curls, and half
The sacred mother's bosom, panting, burst
The laces toward her babe; but she nor cared

Nor knew it, clamouring on, till Ida heard,
Looked up, and rising slowly from me, stood
Erect and silent, striking with her glance
The mother, me, the child; but he that lay
Beside us, Cyril, battered as he was,
Trailed himself up on one knee: then he drew
Her robe to meet his lips, and down she looked
At the armed man sideways, pitying as it seemed,
Or self-involved; but when she learnt his face,
Remembering his ill-omened song, arose
Once more through all her height, and o'er him grew
Tall as a figure lengthened on the sand
When the tide ebbs in sunshine, and he said:

'O fair and strong and terrible! Lioness
That with your long locks play the Lion's mane!
But Love and Nature, these are two more terrible
And stronger. See, your foot is on our necks,
We vanquished, you the Victor of your will.
What would you more? Give her the child! remain
Orbed in your isolation: he is dead,
Or all as dead: henceforth we let you be:
Win you the hearts of women; and beware
Lest, where you seek the common love of these,
The common hate with the revolving wheel
Should drag you down, and some great Nemesis
Break from a darkened future, crowned with fire,
And tread you out for ever: but howso'er
Fixed in yourself, never in your own arms

To hold your own, deny not hers to her,

Give her the child! O if, I say, you keep

One pulse that beats true woman, if you loved

The breast that fed or arm that dandled you,

Or own one port of sense not flint to prayer,

Give her the child! or if you scorn to lay it,

Yourself, in hands so lately claspt with yours,

Or speak to her, your dearest, her one fault,

The tenderness, not yours, that could not kill,

Give me it: I will give it her.

He said:

At first her eye with slow dilation rolled

Dry flame, she listening; after sank and sank

And, into mournful twilight mellowing, dwelt

Full on the child; she took it: 'Pretty bud!

Lily of the vale! half opened bell of the woods!

Sole comfort of my dark hour, when a world

Of traitorous friend and broken system made

No purple in the distance, mystery,

Pledge of a love not to be mine, farewell;

These men are hard upon us as of old,

We two must part: and yet how fain was I

To dream thy cause embraced in mine, to think

I might be something to thee, when I felt

Thy helpless warmth about my barren breast

In the dead prime: but may thy mother prove

As true to thee as false, false, false to me!

And, if thou needs must needs bear the yoke, I wish it

Gentle as freedom'—here she kissed it: then—

'All good go with thee! take it Sir,' and so
Laid the soft babe in his hard-mailèd hands,
Who turned half-round to Psyche as she sprang
To meet it, with an eye that swum in thanks;
Then felt it sound and whole from head to foot,
And hugged and never hugged it close enough,
And in her hunger mouthed and mumbled it,
   And hid her bosom with it; after that
Put on more calm and added suppliantly:

'We two were friends: I go to mine own land
For ever: find some other: as for me
I scarce am fit for your great plans: yet speak to me,
Say one soft word and let me part forgiven.'

But Ida spoke not, rapt upon the child.
Then Arac. 'Ida—'sdeath! you blame the man;
You wrong yourselves—the woman is so hard
Upon the woman. Come, a grace to me!
I am your warrior: I and mine have fought
Your battle: kiss her; take her hand, she weeps:
'Sdeath! I would sooner fight thrice o'er than see it.'

But Ida spoke not, gazing on the ground,
And reddening in the furrows of his chin,
And moved beyond his custom, Gama said:

'I've heard that there is iron in the blood,
And I believe it. Not one word? not one?

Whence drew you this steel temper? not from me,

Not from your mother, now a saint with saints.

She said you had a heart—I heard her say it—

"Our Ida has a heart"—just ere she died—

"But see that some one with authority

Be near her still" and I—I sought for one—

All people said she had authority—

The Lady Blanche: much profit! Not one word;

No! though your father sues: see how you stand

Stiff as Lot's wife, and all the good knights maimed,

I trust that there is no one hurt to death,

For our wild whim: and was it then for this,

Was it for this we gave our palace up,

Where we withdrew from summer heats and state,

And had our wine and chess beneath the planes,

And many a pleasant hour with her that's gone,

Ere you were born to vex us? Is it kind?

Speak to her I say: is this not she of whom,

When first she came, all flushed you said to me

Now had you got a friend of your own age,

Now could you share your thought; now should men see

Two women faster welded in one love

Than pairs of wedlock; she you walked with, she

You talked with, whole nights long, up in the tower,

Of sine and arc, spheroïd and azimuth,

And right ascension, Heaven knows what; and now

A word, but one, one little kindly word,

Not one to spare her: out upon you, flint!

You love nor her, nor me, nor any; nay,

You shame your mother's judgment too. Not one?
You will not? well—no heart have you, or such
As fancies like the vermin in a nut
Have fretted all to dust and bitterness.'
So said the small king moved beyond his wont.

But Ida stood nor spoke, drained of her force
By many a varying influence and so long.
Down through her limbs a drooping languor wept:
Her head a little bent; and on her mouth
A doubtful smile dwelt like a clouded moon
In a still water: then brake out my sire,
Lifted his grim head from my wounds. 'O you,
Woman, whom we thought woman even now,
And were half fooled to let you tend our son,
Because he might have wished it—but we see,
The accomplice of your madness unforgiven,
And think that you might mix his draught with death,
When your skies change again: the rougher hand
Is safer: on to the tents: take up the Prince.'

He rose, and while each ear was pricked to attend
A tempest, through the cloud that dimmed her broke
A genial warmth and light once more, and shone
Through glittering drops on her sad friend.
'Come hither.
O Psyche,' she cried out, 'embrace me, come,
Quick while I melt; make reconcilement sure
With one that cannot keep her mind an hour:

Come to the hollow hear they slander so!
Kiss and be friends, like children being chid!
I seem no more: I want forgiveness too:
I should have had to do with none but maids,
That have no links with men. Ah false but dear,
Dear traitor, too much loved, why?—why?—Yet see,
Before these kings we embrace you yet once more
With all forgiveness, all oblivion,
And trust, not love, you less.
And now, O sire,
Grant me your son, to nurse, to wait upon him,
Like mine own brother. For my debt to him,
This nightmare weight of gratitude, I know it;
Taunt me no more: yourself and yours shall have
Free adit; we will scatter all our maids
Till happier times each to her proper hearth:
What use to keep them here—now? grant my prayer.
Help, father, brother, help; speak to the king:
Thaw this male nature to some touch of that
Which kills me with myself, and drags me down
From my fixt height to mob me up with all
The soft and milky rabble of womankind,
Poor weakling even as they are.'
Passionate tears
Followed: the king replied not: Cyril said:
'Your brother, Lady,—Florian,—ask for him
Of your great head—for he is wounded too—
That you may tend upon him with the prince.'
'Ay so,' said Ida with a bitter smile,

'Our laws are broken: let him enter too.'
Then Violet, she that sang the mournful song,
And had a cousin tumbled on the plain,
Petitioned too for him. 'Ay so,' she said,
'I stagger in the stream: I cannot keep
My heart an eddy from the brawling hour:
We break our laws with ease, but let it be.'
'Ay so?' said Blanche: 'Amazed am I to her
Your Highness: but your Highness breaks with ease
The law your Highness did not make: 'twas I.
I had been wedded wife, I knew mankind,
And blocked them out; but these men came to woo
Your Highness—verily I think to win.'

So she, and turned askance a wintry eye:
But Ida with a voice, that like a bell
Tolled by an earthquake in a trembling tower,
Rang ruin, answered full of grief and scorn.

'Fling our doors wide! all, all, not one, but all,
Not only he, but by my mother's soul,
Whatever man lies wounded, friend or foe,
Shall enter, if he will. Let our girls flit,
Till the storm die! but had you stood by us,
The roar that breaks the Pharos from his base
Had left us rock. She fain would sting us too,
But shall not. Pass, and mingle with your likes.
We brook no further insult but are gone.'
She turned; the very nape of her white neck

Was rosed with indignation: but the Prince
Her brother came; the king her father charmed
Her wounded soul with words: nor did mine own
Refuse her proffer, lastly gave his hand.

Then us they lifted up, dead weights, and bare
Straight to the doors: to them the doors gave way
Groaning, and in the Vestal entry shrieked
The virgin marble under iron heels:
And on they moved and gained the hall, and there
Rested: but great the crush was, and each base,
To left and right, of those tall columns drowned
In silken fluctuation and the swarm
Of female whisperers: at the further end
Was Ida by the throne, the two great cats
Close by her, like supporters on a shield,
Bow-backed with fear: but in the centre stood
The common men with rolling eyes; amazed
They glared upon the women, and aghast
The women stared at these, all silent, save
When armour clashed or jingled, while the day,
Descending, struck athwart the hall, and shot
A flying splendour out of brass and steel,
That o'er the statues leapt from head to head,
Now fired an angry Pallas on the helm,
Now set a wrathful Dian's moon on flame,
And now and then an echo started up,
And shuddering fled from room to room, and died
Of fright in far apartments.

Then the voice

Of Ida sounded, issuing ordinance:

And me they bore up the broad stairs, and through

The long-laid galleries past a hundred doors

To one deep chamber shut from sound, and due

To languid limbs and sickness; left me in it;

And others otherwhere they laid; and all

That afternoon a sound arose of hoof

And chariot, many a maiden passing home

Till happier times; but some were left of those

Held sagest, and the great lords out and in,

From those two hosts that lay beside the walls,

Walked at their will, and everything was changed.

Ask me no more: the moon may draw the sea;

The cloud may stoop from heaven and take the shape

With fold to fold, of mountain or of cape;

But O too fond, when have I answered thee?

Ask me no more.

Ask me no more: what answer should I give?

I love not hollow cheek or faded eye:

Yet, O my friend, I will not have thee die!

Ask me no more, lest I should bid thee live;

Ask me no more.

Ask me no more: thy fate and mine are sealed:

I strove against the stream and all in vain:

Let the great river take me to the main:

No more, dear love, for at a touch I yield;

Ask me no more.

VII

So was their sanctuary violated,
So their fair college turned to hospital;
At first with all confusion: by and by
Sweet order lived again with other laws:
A kindlier influence reigned; and everywhere
Low voices with the ministering hand
Hung round the sick: the maidens came, they talked,
They sang, they read: till she not fair began
To gather light, and she that was, became
Her former beauty treble; and to and fro
With books, with flowers, with Angel offices,
Like creatures native unto gracious act,
And in their own clear element, they moved.

But sadness on the soul of Ida fell,
And hatred of her weakness, blent with shame.
Old studies failed; seldom she spoke: but oft
Clomb to the roofs, and gazed alone for hours
On that disastrous leaguer, swarms of men
Darkening her female field: void was her use,
And she as one that climbs a peak to gaze
O'er land and main, and sees a great black cloud
Drag inward from the deeps, a wall of night,
Blot out the slope of sea from verge to shore,
And suck the blinding splendour from the sand,
And quenching lake by lake and tarn by tarn

Expunge the world: so fared she gazing there;
So blackened all her world in secret, blank
And waste it seemed and vain; till down she came,
And found fair peace once more among the sick.

And twilight dawned; and morn by morn the lark
Shot up and shrilled in flickering gyres, but I
Lay silent in the muffled cage of life:
And twilight gloomed; and broader-grown the bowers
Drew the great night into themselves, and Heaven,
Star after Star, arose and fell; but I,
Deeper than those weird doubts could reach me, lay
Quite sundered from the moving Universe,
Nor knew what eye was on me, nor the hand
That nursed me, more than infants in their sleep.

But Psyche tended Florian: with her oft,
Melissa came; for Blanche had gone, but left
Her child among us, willing she should keep
Court-favour: here and there the small bright head,
A light of healing, glanced about the couch,
Or through the parted silks the tender face
Peeped, shining in upon the wounded man
With blush and smile, a medicine in themselves
To wile the length from languorous hours, and draw
The sting from pain; nor seemed it strange that soon
He rose up whole, and those fair charities
Joined at her side; nor stranger seemed that hears
So gentle, so employed, should close in love,

Than when two dewdrops on the petals shake
To the same sweet air, and tremble deeper down,
And slip at once all-fragrant into one.

Less prosperously the second suit obtained
At first with Psyche. Not though Blanche had sworn
That after that dark night among the fields
She needs must wed him for her own good name;
Not though he built upon the babe restored;
Nor though she liked him, yielded she, but feared
To incense the Head once more; till on a day
When Cyril pleaded, Ida came behind
Seen but of Psyche: on her foot she hung
A moment, and she heard, at which her face
A little flushed, and she past on; but each
Assumed from thence a half-consent involved
In stillness, plighted troth, and were at peace.

Nor only these: Love in the sacred halls
Held carnival at will, and flying struck
With showers of random sweet on maid and man.
Nor did her father cease to press my claim,
Nor did mine own, now reconciled; nor yet
Did those twin-brothers, risen again and whole;
Nor Arac, satiate with his victory.

But I lay still, and with me oft she sat:
Then came a change; for sometimes I would catch
Her hand in wild delirium, gripe it hard,

And fling it like a viper off, and shriek
'You are not Ida;' clasp it once again,
And call her Ida, though I knew her not,
And call her sweet, as if in irony,
And call her hard and cold which seemed a truth:
And still she feared that I should lose my mind,
And often she believed that I should die:
Till out of long frustration of her care,
And pensive tendance in the all-weary noons,
And watches in the dead, the dark, when clocks
Throbbed thunder through the palace floors, or called
On flying Time from all their silver tongues—
And out of memories of her kindlier days,
And sidelong glances at my father's grief,
And at the happy lovers heart in heart—
And out of hauntings of my spoken love,
And lonely listenings to my muttered dream,
And often feeling of the helpless hands,
And wordless broodings on the wasted cheek—
From all a closer interest flourished up,
Tenderness touch by touch, and last, to these,
Love, like an Alpine harebell hung with tears
By some cold morning glacier; frail at first
And feeble, all unconscious of itself,
But such as gathered colour day by day.

Last I woke sane, but well-nigh close to death
For weakness: it was evening: silent light
Slept on the painted walls, wherein were wrought

Two grand designs; for on one side arose
The women up in wild revolt, and stormed
At the Oppian Law. Titanic shapes, they crammed
The forum, and half-crushed among the rest
A dwarf-like Cato cowered. On the other side
Hortensia spoke against the tax; behind,
A train of dames: by axe and eagle sat,
With all their foreheads drawn in Roman scowls,
And half the wolf's-milk curdled in their veins,
The fierce triumvirs; and before them paused
Hortensia pleading: angry was her face.

I saw the forms: I knew not where I was:
They did but look like hollow shows; nor more
Sweet Ida: palm to palm she sat: the dew
Dwelt in her eyes, and softer all her shape
And rounder seemed: I moved: I sighed: a touch
Came round my wrist, and tears upon my hand:
Then all for languor and self-pity ran
Mine down my face, and with what life I had,
And like a flower that cannot all unfold,
So drenched it is with tempest, to the sun,
Yet, as it may, turns toward him, I on her
Fixt my faint eyes, and uttered whisperingly:

'If you be, what I think you, some sweet dream,
I would but ask you to fulfil yourself:
But if you be that Ida whom I knew,
I ask you nothing: only, if a dream,

Sweet dream, be perfect. I shall die tonight.
Stoop down and seem to kiss me ere I die.'

I could no more, but lay like one in trance,
That hears his burial talked of by his friends,
And cannot speak, nor move, nor make one sign,
But lies and dreads his doom. She turned; she paused;
She stooped; and out of languor leapt a cry;
Leapt fiery Passion from the brinks of death;
And I believed that in the living world
My spirit closed with Ida's at the lips;
Till back I fell, and from mine arms she rose
Glowing all over noble shame; and all
Her falser self slipt from her like a robe,
And left her woman, lovelier in her mood
Than in her mould that other, when she came
From barren deeps to conquer all with love;
And down the streaming crystal dropt; and she
Far-fleeted by the purple island-sides,
Naked, a double light in air and wave,
To meet her Graces, where they decked her out
For worship without end; nor end of mine,
Stateliest, for thee! but mute she glided forth,
Nor glanced behind her, and I sank and slept,
Filled through and through with Love, a happy sleep.

Deep in the night I woke: she, near me, held
A volume of the Poets of her land:
There to herself, all in low tones, she read.

'Now sleeps the crimson petal, now the white;
Nor waves the cypress in the palace walk;
Nor winks the gold fin in the porphyry font:
The fire-fly wakens: wake thou with me.

Now droops the milkwhite peacock like a ghost,
And like a ghost she glimmers on to me.

Now lies the Earth all Danaë to the stars,
And all thy heart lies open unto me.

Now lies the silent meteor on, and leaves
A shining furrow, as thy thoughts in me.

Now folds the lily all her sweetness up,
And slips into the bosom of the lake:
So fold thyself, my dearest, thou, and slip
Into my bosom and be lost in me.'
I heard her turn the page; she found a small
Sweet Idyl, and once more, as low, she read:
'Come down, O maid, from yonder mountain height:
What pleasure lives in height (the shepherd sang)
In height and cold, the splendour of the hills?
But cease to move so near the Heavens, and cease
To glide a sunbeam by the blasted Pine,
To sit a star upon the sparkling spire;
And come, for love is of the valley, come,
For love is of the valley, come thou down
And find him; by the happy threshold, he,

Or hand in hand with Plenty in the maize,

Or red with spirted purple of the vats,

Or foxlike in the vine; nor cares to walk

With Death and Morning on the silver horns,

Nor wilt thou snare him in the white ravine,

Nor find him dropt upon the firths of ice,

That huddling slant in furrow-cloven falls

To roll the torrent out of dusky doors:

But follow; let the torrent dance thee down

To find him in the valley; let the wild

Lean-headed Eagles yelp alone, and leave

The monstrous ledges there to slope, and spill

Their thousand wreaths of dangling water-smoke,

That like a broken purpose waste in air:

So waste not thou; but come; for all the vales

Await thee; azure pillars of the hearth

Arise to thee; the children call, and I

Thy shepherd pipe, and sweet is every sound,

Sweeter thy voice, but every sound is sweet;

Myriads of rivulets hurrying through the lawn,

The moan of doves in immemorial elms,

And murmuring of innumerable bees.'

So she low-toned; while with shut eyes I lay

Listening; then looked. Pale was the perfect face;

The bosom with long sighs laboured; and meek

Seemed the full lips, and mild the luminous eyes,

And the voice trembled and the hand. She said

Brokenly, that she knew it, she had failed

In sweet humility; had failed in all;

That all her labour was but as a block
Left in the quarry; but she still were loth,
She still were loth to yield herself to one
That wholly scorned to help their equal rights
Against the sons of men, and barbarous laws.
She prayed me not to judge their cause from her
That wronged it, sought far less for truth than power
In knowledge: something wild within her breast,
A greater than all knowledge, beat her down.
And she had nursed me there from week to week:
Much had she learnt in little time. In part
It was ill counsel had misled the girl
To vex true hearts: yet was she but a girl—
'Ah fool, and made myself a Queen of farce!
When comes another such? never, I think,
Till the Sun drop, dead, from the signs.'
Her voice
choked, and her forehead sank upon her hands,
And her great heart through all the faultful Past
Went sorrowing in a pause I dared not break;
Till notice of a change in the dark world
Was lispt about the acacias, and a bird,
That early woke to feed her little ones,
Sent from a dewy breast a cry for light:
She moved, and at her feet the volume fell.

'Blame not thyself too much,' I said, 'nor blame
Too much the sons of men and barbarous laws;
These were the rough ways of the world till now.

Henceforth thou hast a helper, me, that know
The woman's cause is man's: they rise or sink
Together, dwarfed or godlike, bond or free:
For she that out of Lethe scales with man
The shining steps of Nature, shares with man
His nights, his days, moves with him to one goal,
Stays all the fair young planet in her hands—
If she be small, slight-natured, miserable,
How shall men grow? but work no more alone!
Our place is much: as far as in us lies
We two will serve them both in aiding her—
Will clear away the parasitic forms
That seem to keep her up but drag her down—
Will leave her space to burgeon out of all
Within her—let her make herself her own
To give or keep, to live and learn and be
All that not harms distinctive womanhood.
For woman is not undevelopt man,
But diverse: could we make her as the man,
Sweet Love were slain: his dearest bond is this,
Not like to like, but like in difference.
Yet in the long years liker must they grow;
The man be more of woman, she of man;
He gain in sweetness and in moral height,
Nor lose the wrestling thews that throw the world;
She mental breadth, nor fail in childward care,
Nor lose the childlike in the larger mind;
Till at the last she set herself to man,
Like perfect music unto noble words;

And so these twain, upon the skirts of Time,

Sit side by side, full-summed in all their powers,

Dispensing harvest, sowing the To-be,

Self-reverent each and reverencing each,

Distinct in individualities,

But like each other even as those who love.

Then comes the statelier Eden back to men:

Then reign the world's great bridals, chaste and calm:

Then springs the crowning race of humankind.

May these things be!'

Sighing she spoke 'I fear

They will not.'

'Dear, but let us type them now

In our own lives, and this proud watchword rest

Of equal; seeing either sex alone

Is half itself, and in true marriage lies

Nor equal, nor unequal: each fulfils

Defect in each, and always thought in thought,

Purpose in purpose, will in will, they grow,

The single pure and perfect animal,

The two-celled heart beating, with one full stroke,

Life.'

And again sighing she spoke: 'A dream

That once was mine! what woman taught you this?'

'Alone,' I said, 'from earlier than I know,

Immersed in rich foreshadowings of the world,

I loved the woman: he, that doth not, lives

A drowning life, besotted in sweet self,

Or pines in sad experience worse than death,
Or keeps his winged affections clipt with crime:
Yet was there one through whom I loved her, one
Not learnèd, save in gracious household ways,
Not perfect, nay, but full of tender wants,
No Angel, but a dearer being, all dipt
In Angel instincts, breathing Paradise,
Interpreter between the Gods and men,
Who looked all native to her place, and yet
On tiptoe seemed to touch upon a sphere
Too gross to tread, and all male minds perforce
Swayed to her from their orbits as they moved,
And girdled her with music. Happy he
With such a mother! faith in womankind
Beats with his blood, and trust in all things high
Comes easy to him, and though he trip and fall
He shall not blind his soul with clay.'
                    'But I,'
Said Ida, tremulously, 'so all unlike—
It seems you love to cheat yourself with words:
This mother is your model. I have heard
of your strange doubts: they well might be: I seem
A mockery to my own self. Never, Prince;
            You cannot love me.'
            'Nay but thee' I said
'From yearlong poring on thy pictured eyes,
Ere seen I loved, and loved thee seen, and saw
Thee woman through the crust of iron moods
That masked thee from men's reverence up, and forced

Sweet love on pranks of saucy boyhood: now,
Given back to life, to life indeed, through thee,
Indeed I love: the new day comes, the light
Dearer for night, as dearer thou for faults
Lived over: lift thine eyes; my doubts are dead,
My haunting sense of hollow shows: the change,
This truthful change in thee has killed it. Dear,
Look up, and let thy nature strike on mine,
Like yonder morning on the blind half-world;
Approach and fear not; breathe upon my brows;
In that fine air I tremble, all the past
Melts mist-like into this bright hour, and this
Is morn to more, and all the rich to-come
Reels, as the golden Autumn woodland reels
Athwart the smoke of burning weeds. Forgive me,
I waste my heart in signs: let be. My bride,
My wife, my life. O we will walk this world,
Yoked in all exercise of noble end,
And so through those dark gates across the wild
That no man knows. Indeed I love thee: come,
Yield thyself up: my hopes and thine are one:
Accomplish thou my manhood and thyself;
Lay thy sweet hands in mine and trust to me.'

CONCLUSION

So closed our tale, of which I give you all

The random scheme as wildly as it rose:

The words are mostly mine; for when we ceased

There came a minute's pause, and Walter said,

'I wish she had not yielded!' then to me,

'What, if you drest it up poetically?'

So prayed the men, the women: I gave assent:

Yet how to bind the scattered scheme of seven

Together in one sheaf? What style could suit?

The men required that I should give throughout

The sort of mock-heroic gigantesque,

With which we bantered little Lilia first:

The women—and perhaps they felt their power,

For something in the ballads which they sang,

Or in their silent influence as they sat,

Had ever seemed to wrestle with burlesque,

And drove us, last, to quite a solemn close—

They hated banter, wished for something real,

A gallant fight, a noble princess—why

Not make her true-heroic—true-sublime?

Or all, they said, as earnest as the close?

Which yet with such a framework scarce could be.

Then rose a little feud betwixt the two,

Betwixt the mockers and the realists:

And I, betwixt them both, to please them both,

And yet to give the story as it rose,

I moved as in a strange diagonal,
And maybe neither pleased myself nor them.

But Lilia pleased me, for she took no part
In our dispute: the sequel of the tale
Had touched her; and she sat, she plucked the grass,
She flung it from her, thinking: last, she fixt
A showery glance upon her aunt, and said,
'You—tell us what we are' who might have told,
For she was crammed with theories out of books,
But that there rose a shout: the gates were closed
At sunset, and the crowd were swarming now,
To take their leave, about the garden rails.

So I and some went out to these: we climbed
The slope to Vivian-place, and turning saw
The happy valleys, half in light, and half
Far-shadowing from the west, a land of peace;
Gray halls alone among their massive groves;
Trim hamlets; here and there a rustic tower
Half-lost in belts of hop and breadths of wheat;
The shimmering glimpses of a stream; the seas;
A red sail, or a white; and far beyond,
Imagined more than seen, the skirts of France.

'Look there, a garden!' said my college friend,
The Tory member's elder son, 'and there!
God bless the narrow sea which keeps her off,
And keeps our Britain, whole within herself,

A nation yet, the rulers and the ruled—
Some sense of duty, something of a faith,
Some reverence for the laws ourselves have made,
Some patient force to change them when we will,
Some civic manhood firm against the crowd—
But yonder, whiff! there comes a sudden heat,
The gravest citizen seems to lose his head,
The king is scared, the soldier will not fight,
The little boys begin to shoot and stab,
A kingdom topples over with a shriek
Like an old woman, and down rolls the world
In mock heroics stranger than our own;
Revolts, republics, revolutions, most
No graver than a schoolboys' barring out;
Too comic for the serious things they are,
Too solemn for the comic touches in them,
Like our wild Princess with as wise a dream
As some of theirs—God bless the narrow seas!
I wish they were a whole Atlantic broad.'

'Have patience,' I replied, 'ourselves are full
Of social wrong; and maybe wildest dreams
Are but the needful preludes of the truth:
For me, the genial day, the happy crowd,
The sport half-science, fill me with a faith.
This fine old world of ours is but a child
Yet in the go-cart. Patience! Give it time
To learn its limbs: there is a hand that guides.'

In such discourse we gained the garden rails,
And there we saw Sir Walter where he stood,
Before a tower of crimson holly-hoaks,
Among six boys, head under head, and looked
No little lily-handed Baronet he,
A great broad-shouldered genial Englishman,
A lord of fat prize-oxen and of sheep,
A raiser of huge melons and of pine,
A patron of some thirty charities,
A pamphleteer on guano and on grain,
A quarter-sessions chairman, abler none;
Fair-haired and redder than a windy morn;
Now shaking hands with him, now him, of those
That stood the nearest—now addressed to speech—
Who spoke few words and pithy, such as closed
Welcome, farewell, and welcome for the year
To follow: a shout rose again, and made
The long line of the approaching rookery swerve
From the elms, and shook the branches of the deer
From slope to slope through distant ferns, and rang
Beyond the bourn of sunset; O, a shout
More joyful than the city-roar that hails
Premier or king! Why should not these great Sirs
Give up their parks some dozen times a year
To let the people breathe? So thrice they cried,
I likewise, and in groups they streamed away.

But we went back to the Abbey, and sat on,
So much the gathering darkness charmed: we sat

But spoke not, rapt in nameless reverie,
Perchance upon the future man: the walls
Blackened about us, bats wheeled, and owls whooped,
And gradually the powers of the night,
That range above the region of the wind,
Deepening the courts of twilight broke them up
Through all the silent spaces of the worlds,
Beyond all thought into the Heaven of Heavens.

Last little Lilia, rising quietly,
Disrobed the glimmering statue of Sir Ralph
From those rich silks, and home well-pleased we went.

Milton Keynes UK
Ingram Content Group UK Ltd.
UKHW030719041024
449263UK00004B/371

9 789362 093097